ERP Revolution: Transforming the Future of Business

Unleashing the Path to Business Excellence and Competitive Advantage for the Digital Age

(ISBN: 978-93-95470-65-0)

Dr. Amol S Kalgaonkar

M.E. (Computer), Ph.D.
amolkalgaonkar@hotmail.com

Copyright © 2023 Book Saga Publications.

ERP Revolution: Transforming the Future of Business

All rights reserved. This book or any portion thereof may not be reproduced or used in any manner whatsoever without the express written permission of the publisher except for the use of brief quotation in a book review. The views and results expressed in various articles are those of the authors and not of editors or publisher of the book.

ISBN: 978-93-95470-65-0

Dr. Amol S Kalgaonkar

Published by: Book Saga Publications

Rahuri Factory, Rahuri, Ahmednagar, Maharashtra, India, 413706.

Website - www.booksagapublications.com

E-mail - contact@booksagapublications.com

Mobile- +918788403871

First Edition - 15th July 2023

Dedication

To my beloved family,

To my remarkable wife, Anjali thank you for your unwavering belief in me and for being my constant companion in both triumphs and challenges. To my beautiful children, Deven and Shruti, you are my motivation and the light that brightens my path. Your infectious curiosity and boundless energy remind me of the importance of innovation and the endless possibilities that lie ahead. May this book inspire you to dream big and embrace the world of enterprise technologies fearlessly.

To my extraordinary parents, who are the unwavering pillars of love and guidance, Your selfless devotion knows no bounds, You have nurtured with tender care, Your sacrifices and unwavering support have shaped my paths forever.

To my In-laws, siblings, brother-in-laws, sister-in-law, nieces and nephew, thank you for instilling in me a love for learning, perseverance, and the pursuit of excellence. Your guidance and encouragement have shaped me into the person I am today, and I am forever indebted to your unwavering belief in me.

This book is dedicated to all of you, as a token of my deepest gratitude. Your love and support have been the driving force behind my endeavours, and I am truly blessed to have you by my side. May this dedication serve as a testament to the immeasurable love and appreciation I hold for each and every one of you.

With all my love, Amol

Contents

FOREWORD I
PREFACE II
ACKNOWLEDGMENTS III
INTRODUCTION IV

1 1

INTRODUCTION TO ERP 1
    Introduction 1
    History and Evolution 2
    Definition and Concept of ERP 6
    Geo Political situations and ERP 7
    Advantages of ERP 9
    Disadvantages of ERP 14
    Applicability of ERP 18

2 23

OVERVIEW OF ENTERPRISE 23
    Introduction 23
    Definition of Enterprise 24
    Types of enterprises 26
    Challenges facing enterprises 29
    Need of ERP for enterprises 32
    Integration of Management Information System 34
    Modelling Business with Information Systems 38
    The Integrated Data Model (IDM) 41
    Objectives of ERP 44
    Types of ERP 47

3 55

ERP — A Manufacturing Perspective 55
Introduction to ERP in Manufacturing 55
Material Requirement Planning (MRP) 56
Manufacturing Resource Planning-II (MRP-II) 58
Distribution Requirement Planning (DRP) 61
Just-In-Time (JIT) and Kanban System 62
Process Management 64
Work Management 66
Workflow Management 68
Work History Management 70
Product Data Management (PDM) 72

4 78

ERP and Related Technologies 78
Introduction 78
Business Process Reengineering 79
Data Warehousing 82
Data Mining 84
Supply Chain Management 86
Customer Relationship Management 89

5 92

Components of ERP systems 92
Introduction 92
Enterprise-wide database 93
Business process automation 96
Integration of functional areas 99
Reporting and analytics 102

6 120

ERP implementation process 120
Introduction 120
Pre-evaluation screening 121
ERP Package evaluation 126
Project planning and management 128

  Business process mapping and re-engineering 130
  Configuration 132
  Testing 134
  User training 135
  Going live 136
  Post-implementation (maintenance mode) 137
  Challenges and risks of ERP implementation 139

7 148

COMMON ERP MODULES AND THEIR FUNCTIONS 148
 Introduction 148
  1. *Finance Modules* 149
  2. *Sales and Distribution Modules* 150
  3. *Manufacturing Modules* 151
  4. *Human Resources Modules* 153
  5. *Plant Maintenance Modules* 155
  6. *Quality Management Modules* 156
  7. *Materials Management* 158

8 161

ERP CUSTOMIZATION AND INTEGRATION 161
 Introduction 161
 Customizing ERP to meet business needs 164
 Integrating ERP with other software applications 166
 In-house Implementation – Pros and Cons 169
 Vendors: Role of the Vendor 172
 Consultants: Role of Consultants 174
 End-Users 177

9 180

ERP MARKET 180
 Introduction to the ERP market 180
 Current state of the ERP market 182
 Major ERP vendors and their offerings 185
 ERP for different industries 189
 ERP for different business sizes 191
 Cloud-based ERP vs On-premise ERP 193

  Implementation costs and factors affecting them 197
  ERP trends and future outlook 199

10 202

FUTURE OF ERP 202
  Introduction 202
  Historical evolution of ERP technology 203
  Current state of the ERP market 203
  Emerging trends in ERP technology 205
  Potential impact of emerging technologies on ERP systems 208
  Future of ERP implementation and maintenance 209
  ERP systems for Industry 4.0 210
  ERP systems for sustainable business practices 211
  Challenges and opportunities for ERP vendors and users in the future
  .. 212
  Conclusion and outlook 213

11 215

FACTORS AFFECTING ERP PROJECT SUCCESS 215
  Introduction 215
  Project Planning and Management 217
  Stakeholder Engagement 217
  Organizational Readiness 217
  Change Management 218
  Technical Considerations 218
  Vendor Selection and Collaboration 219
  Lessons Learned from Failed ERP Projects 219
  Success Stories and Best Practices 219
  Conclusion and Outlook 220
REFERENCES 221

Foreword

In the dynamic and ever-evolving world of business, the effective management of operations is essential for success. In the book "ERP Revolution: Transforming the future of Business" (Unleashing the Path to Business Excellence and Competitive Advantage for the Digital Age), the esteemed author takes us on a journey into the realm of Enterprise Resource Planning (ERP) systems and their profound impact on organizational performance. With deep expertise and a wealth of industry knowledge, the author explores how ERP systems have become indispensable tools for businesses, enabling them to streamline operations, enhance efficiency, and make data-driven decisions.

This book serves as a compelling introduction to the author's work, offering valuable insights into why ERP systems have emerged as a transformative force in the modern business landscape. It not only emphasizes the relevance and timeliness of the book's content but also highlights the author's expertise and their significant contributions to the field. This book captures readers' attention, sparking their curiosity and inspiring them to explore the transformative potential of ERP for achieving business excellence and gaining a competitive edge. Whether you are a business leader, an aspiring professional, or an industry enthusiast, this book will undoubtedly equip you with the knowledge and insights needed to navigate the intricacies of ERP systems and unleash their full potential in transforming business operations.

Mark Westraad
Date: 10th March, 2023.

Preface

In today's competitive business environment, businesses need to be able to operate efficiently and effectively in order to succeed. Enterprise resource planning (ERP) systems can help businesses to do just that. ERP systems integrate all of a company's core business processes, such as accounting, manufacturing, sales, and customer service, into a single system. This integration can help businesses to improve efficiency, reduce costs, and improve decision-making.

This book provides a comprehensive overview of ERP systems. It covers the benefits of ERP, the different types of ERP systems, the selection process, and the implementation process. The book also includes factors which are helpful for ERP project success.

This book is an essential resource for any business that is considering implementing an ERP system. It provides the knowledge and tools you need to make the process a success.

Dr Amol S Kalgaonkar
Date: 2nd April, 2023.

Acknowledgments

I would like to extend my heartfelt gratitude and appreciation to the individuals who have contributed to the creation of "ERP Revolution: Transforming the Future of Business" (Unleashing the Path to Business Excellence and Competitive Advantage for the Digital Age).

I would like to express my sincere thanks to all my colleagues who have worked with me in this ERP implementation field for past twenty-five years. All the insightful feedback and constructive suggestions have greatly enhanced the quality of this book. Their contributions, including research assistance and thoughtful discussions, have significantly enriched the content of this book.

I would also like to acknowledge the contributions of the professionals who generously shared their expertise during the interviews conducted for this book. Their insights and experiences have added depth and authenticity to the narratives.

I would like to thank the publishing team at Book Saga Publications, Ahmednagar for their dedication and hard work in bringing this book to life. Their professionalism and attention to detail have been instrumental in the successful completion of this project.

Lastly, I would like to thank my parents, my wife Anjali, children Deven and Shruti for their love and support during the writing of this book. Their love and belief in me have been the driving force behind this accomplishment.

To all those mentioned above and many others who have played a part in this book's creation, thank you for your invaluable contributions and support. Your involvement has made this endeavor possible, and I am truly grateful.

Introduction

Enterprise resource planning (ERP) systems are integrated software suites that help businesses to manage their core business processes, such as accounting, manufacturing, sales, and customer service. ERP systems can help businesses to improve efficiency, reduce costs, and improve decision-making.

This book provides a comprehensive overview of ERP systems. It covers the benefits of ERP, the different types of ERP systems, the selection process, and the implementation process. The book also includes case studies of successful ERP implementations.

Chapters in this book provides readers with a comprehensive overview of the book's content and structure, giving them a glimpse into the key topics and concepts. From understanding the fundamental principles of ERP to exploring its implications in various industries, readers will gain valuable insights into the manufacturing perspective, related technologies, and the components that comprise ERP systems.

The book highlights the significance of the ERP implementation process, common modules and their functions, customization and integration aspects, as well as the current market trends and the future outlook for ERP.

With a focus on uncovering the factors that can impact the success of ERP projects, this book sets the stage for an enriching exploration of ERP's transformative potential in achieving business excellence and gaining a competitive advantage.

1

Introduction to ERP

The way businesses operate has been fundamentally transformed by ERP (Enterprise Resource Planning) systems, which bring together several functional areas into a coherent and efficient framework. In today's fast-paced and fiercely competitive corporate environment, organisations rely on ERP to optimise their processes, maximise resource utilisation, and promote growth.

A complete overview of ERP is provided in this introduction chapter, establishing the framework for a more in-depth analysis of its complexity and practical applications. It examines the origins and development of ERP while highlighting its revolutionary impact on current business operations. By understanding the basic ideas and benefits of the system, readers will get insights into how ERP helps firms achieve operational excellence and negotiate the complexities of a rapidly changing industry.

Throughout this book, we will examine the implementation, personalization, integration, and potential uses of ERP.

Introduction

Welcome to the world of enterprise resource planning (ERP), a comprehensive method for managing enterprises that has revolutionised how companies operate and thrive in the current, fast-paced economy. We set out on a mission to examine the fundamental concepts, distinctive traits, and extensive benefits of ERP in this introductory chapter.

Finance, supply chain, human resources, and customer relationship management may all be integrated into one cohesive corporate operation with the help of ERP. Processes are simplified, data visibility is enhanced, and decision-makers are given real-time insights, enabling businesses to achieve operational excellence and promote sustainable growth.

We go into the complexities of ERP in this book, covering setup, customization, and integration. Prior to getting into the specifics, it's critical to have a firm grasp of how ERP works and how it has developed. We give a thorough overview, detailing its beginnings, historical backdrop, and important elements that have helped it develop into a ground-breaking commercial solution. Readers can learn a lot about the development of ERP as well as the revolutionary ideas that have influenced it.

In addition, we highlight the core features and benefits of ERP, showcasing its ability to boost productivity, streamline processes, and facilitate informed decision-making. Understanding these fundamental concepts will serve as a foundation for delving into the more complex aspects of ERP deployment, customization, and integration discussed in the subsequent chapters.

History and Evolution

ERP systems have changed how firms manage their resources and operations throughout time. To understand the current status of ERP, we must look back on its past and chart its development from humble beginnings to its complex and modern form.

The concept of integrated computer-based systems for business administration first emerged in the 1960s and 1970s. Around this time, businesses began employing mainframe computers to automate processes like accounting and inventory management and control. These early systems lacked the complete integration that differentiates contemporary ERP and had a limited scope.

The true innovation came with the introduction of Material Requirements Planning (MRP) systems in the 1970s. MRP gave businesses a structured way to manage their manufacturing resources by concentrating on production schedule optimisation and inventory management. MRP was a tremendous advancement, but it was limited to the manufacturing sector and did not include other corporate activities.

Building on the success of MRP, Manufacturing Resource Planning II (MRP II) systems were created in the 1980s. MRP II expanded the use of MRP by including other commercial activities outside manufacturing. It established a connection between materials planning and other operational elements including shop floor management, capacity planning, and financial management. Businesses may more effectively match output with demand and manage resources thanks to MRP II's comprehensive approach to enterprise-wide resource planning.

The true birth of ERP occurred in the 1990s when software engineers discovered the necessity for integrated systems that could manage numerous functional areas within enterprises. MRP II provided the foundation for the creation of ERP systems, whose applications have now expanded to cover essential company functions including finance, human resources, sales, and distribution. This complete integration allowed for the smooth information flow, real-time data visibility, and improved decision-making.

Early ERP systems were expensive and complicated, primarily serving large companies. ERP became more scalable and available thanks to developments in computing technologies like client-server architecture and relational databases. Because of this, ERP solutions have developed throughout time to support companies of all sizes and have increased their capabilities to support more industries.

When the internet and cloud technologies first appeared, ERP underwent a huge shift. The history of ERP underwent a transformation in the 2000s with the introduction of web features and Internet-based ERP (ERP II). The accessibility and usability of ERP systems were further improved by users being able to access ERP functionalities through standard web browsers thanks to web technologies and web-based interfaces.

An important turning point in the evolution of ERP systems was the introduction of cloud-based ERP solutions. By enabling scalable and on-demand access to resources over the internet, cloud computing completely changed the IT environment in the 2010s. ERP solutions that were cloud-based offered improved flexibility, scalability, and affordability. Remote access to ERP features allowed businesses to streamline maintenance procedures and do away with the requirement for significant infrastructure investments.

Resource management and corporate operations have undergone a revolution thanks to ERP. ERP systems have developed into comprehensive solutions that combine and improve many company activities from their initial design to automating manufacturing processes. This shift has been fueled by technological development and changing business needs. To meet the ever-increasing demands of the business world, organisations can now use ERP systems to streamline operations, improve collaboration, and make data-driven choices. The quest for productivity, efficiency, and adaptability in a fast-paced business environment has been the impetus behind the development of ERP.

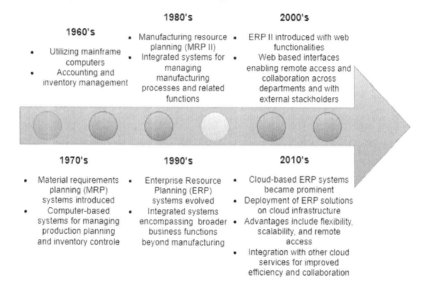

Figure 1. Evolution of ERP: A Historical Timeline

A timeline of the significant turning points in the development and history of ERP systems is shown in Fig. 1.

ERP has made significant strides and important turning points along the way, extending its functional reach to include important divisions like sales, distribution, and finance. The efficiency, scalability, and capacities of ERP systems have been significantly improved because to technological advancement. Additionally, the introduction of the internet and cloud computing has ushered in a new era of change for ERP by offering remote access, mobile compatibility, and affordable deployment alternatives. These innovations have revolutionised the use and adaptability of ERP, driving businesses towards more reliable and adaptable operations.

Industry-specific ERP systems have arisen to meet the specific needs of numerous industries, including manufacturing, healthcare, retail, and finance. The importance of user experience and flexibility has increased, motivating providers to make investments in enhancing user interfaces, navigation, and customization possibilities. The adoption of cutting-edge technology like artificial intelligence (AI), machine learning (ML), the Internet of Things (IoT), and predictive analytics is anticipated for ERP in the future. These developments will improve automation, allow for informed choice-making, and offer data-driven insights, empowering businesses to streamline operations and promote expansion.

ERP has established itself as a key component of contemporary corporate management, allowing businesses to streamline processes, combine activities, and gather in-depth company knowledge. ERP has consistently developed and impacted the way organisations function in a complex and interconnected environment, starting with its early days with Inventory Management System and MRP to the broad and sophisticated systems of today.

Definition and Concept of ERP

ERP is a comprehensive piece of software that combines several organisational processes and commercial activities. By acting as a focal point, it promotes the smooth transfer of information and resources between departments, promoting effective planning, teamwork, and decision-making. ERP offers a comprehensive perspective of organisational operations thanks to its vast features and modules covering finance, human resources, manufacturing, supply chain management, sales, and more. ERP gives insightful data for data-driven strategy planning by combining data from several domains onto a single platform.

Definition: ERP is a complete software program that links many internal company processes. It acts as a focal point, facilitating the efficient transfer of data and resources between divisions and fostering effective planning, teamwork, and decision-making. ERP offers a comprehensive perspective of organisational operations with its wide range of functions and modules, including finance, human resources, manufacturing, supply chain management, sales, and more. ERP provides a complete viewpoint and allows data-driven insights for strategic planning by combining data from several business domains into a single platform.

ERP systems are made to improve and streamline corporate processes by getting rid of extraneous chores, using less manual labour, and increasing productivity. ERP enables businesses to efficiently allocate resources, cut costs, and increase overall efficiency by automating routine operations and workflows. ERP provides managers with invaluable insights into key performance indicators (KPIs) through real-time monitoring and reporting capabilities, enabling educated decision-making and prompt measures to promote success.

ERP was developed as a response to the shortcomings of various software applications and manual processes in organisations. ERP improved organisational efficiency by streamlining processes, encouraging collaboration, and merging many tasks onto a single platform. Companies used separate systems for managing customer databases, inventories, and accounting prior to the advent of ERP, which resulted in data silos and unnecessary duplication of work. ERP systems boost productivity and strategic planning by automating repetitive operations, providing real-time information, and assisting informed decision-making.

Geo Political situations and ERP

Numerous geopolitical events happened concurrently with the creation and development of ERP principles. Here are a few notable examples:

1. Globalisation and the Cold War: ERP systems started to take shape in the 1960s and 1970s, at the height of the Cold War. There is an increasing need for integrated systems to manage resources and operations due to rising globalisation and the growth of multinational organisations. ERP systems were created to improve worldwide business operations and streamline processes in response to evolving global business needs.
2. Economic Integration in Europe: ERP principles were developed in response to the demand for standardised business practises and procedures as a result of the economic union of Europe through the EEC and EU. ERP systems were essential in coordinating business operations and maintaining compliance with EU rules when trade restrictions were abolished and a single market was established.
3. Global Economic Shifts: The development of ERP concepts coincided with major changes in the world economy. For instance, as manufacturing and service centres, rising economies like China and India have grown, there is a greater need for ERP systems to control intricate supply chains and international business operations. Resource planning and management systems that were effective were required due to the expanding interconnection of international markets and the expansion of multinational organisations, which ERP supplied.
4. Geopolitical Competition and Technological Advances: The development of ERP concepts was significantly influenced by technological advancement, notably in the fields of computing, networking, and telecommunications. During times of geopolitical confrontation, such as the Space Race between the United States and the Soviet Union, the race for

technological dominance sparked innovation in computer and data processing technology. These developments laid the groundwork for the birth of ERP systems and the development that followed.

Geopolitical circumstances may not have had a direct impact on the fundamental ideas of ERP, but they have had an impact on the larger corporate context in which ERP systems have evolved. The demand for ERP solutions has been impacted by elements including globalisation, economic integration, shifting power dynamics, and technical improvements, which have also had an impact on the implementation methods of organisations.

Advantages of ERP

Businesses can acquire a competitive edge and overcome a variety of obstacles in today's changing industry by deploying an ERP system. Let's examine the many advantages that ERP offers, enabling businesses to improve efficiency, streamline procedures, and accomplish strategic goals. ERP provides a broad range of benefits that pave the way for sustained growth and success, from increased operational efficiency to improved decision-making abilities.

It is crucial to emphasise the following elements while discussing the benefits of ERP systems:

1. Integrated Information: ERP systems provide accurate and real-time information by combining data from many departments and functions into a single database. By giving a comprehensive perspective of the organisation, this integration enhances data integrity, removes data duplication, and facilitates improved decision-making.
2. Streamlined Processes: The automation and simplification of corporate processes using ERP systems reduces the need

for manual labour, paperwork, and unnecessary jobs. Organisations can increase production, improve response times, and improve overall operational efficiency by removing bottlenecks and inefficiencies.
3. Enhanced Departmental and Functional Collaboration and Communication: ERP fosters departmental and functional collaboration and communication. Employee collaboration and information sharing are both made possible by this. This promotes collaboration, dismantles silos, and makes it easier to coordinate, which boosts organisational effectiveness and customer happiness.
4. Better Customer Relationship Management (CRM): ERP systems frequently come with CRM modules that assist businesses in managing interactions with and relationships with their customers. Organisations may improve customer service, personalise interactions, and obtain insights to create a better customer experience by centralising customer data. This boosts client retention, customer happiness, and sales prospects.
5. Reporting and Data Visibility: ERP systems offer extensive reporting and data visibility features. Users may create customised reports, view real-time dashboards, and do data analysis to learn important lessons about how well their businesses are performing. This provides accurate and timely information to decision-makers, empowering them to take well-informed decisions and lead strategic initiatives.
6. Cost Savings: By streamlining operations, lowering manual errors, lowering the cost of carrying inventory, and enhancing supply chain management, ERP systems can help reduce expenses. Organisations can save costs and maximise resource utilisation by simplifying operations and improving efficiency.

7. Flexibility and Scalability: ERP systems are created to scale as businesses expand. They offer adaptability to accommodate new processes, adjust to shifting business requirements, and integrate more modules or features. The ERP system can adapt to the changing needs of the organisation thanks to its scalability and flexibility, supporting its long-term growth and expansion.
8. ERP systems frequently include capabilities to make regulatory compliance easier, especially in sectors with strict reporting and regulatory requirements. These technologies help organisations comply with legal and regulatory requirements by automating compliance procedures, ensuring data quality and correctness, and generating audit trails.
9. Enhanced Data Security: To secure sensitive data, ERP systems frequently have strong security measures. ERP systems assist in preventing unauthorised access and data breaches by using role-based access restrictions, encryption, and user authentication procedures.
10. Efficient Resource Management: ERP systems enable organizations to effectively manage their resources, including materials, inventory, equipment, and human capital. By optimizing resource allocation and utilization, organizations can reduce waste, minimize inventory costs, and improve workforce productivity.
11. Standardisation and Best Practises: By imposing uniform procedures and practises throughout the organisation, ERP systems foster standardisation. This guarantees that processes adhere to established workflows, resulting in increased effectiveness, decreased error rates, and greater quality control. ERP systems frequently include industry

best practises, giving businesses access to tried-and-true benchmarks and processes.
12. Analytics and Business Intelligence: ERP systems can offer strong analytics and business intelligence capabilities. Organisations can obtain important insights into key performance indicators, trends, and patterns by utilising data gathered within the ERP system. This makes it possible to make data-driven decisions, plan proactively, and find ways to cut costs and enhance processes.
13. Global Operations and Multi-site Management: ERP solutions provide centralised control and visibility for businesses with worldwide operations or many locations. ERP systems provide effective management of operations across globally distributed sites by supporting multiple languages and currencies, intercompany transactions, and global reporting capabilities.
14. Integration of the supply chain and vendors: ERP systems frequently have functionality for integrating the supply chain, managing vendors, and purchasing. These features help businesses speed contacts with suppliers, improve supplier relationship management, track orders, manage contracts, and optimise procurement procedures. This integration results in improved inventory management, shorter lead times, and more seamless supply chain processes.
15. Competitive Advantage: Putting in place an ERP system can give businesses a competitive edge in the marketplace. Organisations may stand out from rivals, react rapidly to market changes, and seize new business possibilities by improving operational efficiency, customer happiness, and strategic decision-making.

16. Enhanced Reporting and Analytics: With the help of ERP systems' sophisticated reporting and analytics capabilities, businesses can create individualised dashboards, reports, and analytics to measure key performance indicators (KPIs) and make progress towards objectives. By giving managers and executives rapid access to correct information, they are better equipped to make wise decisions.
17. Integration with Other Software and Third-Party Systems: ERP systems are able to integrate with other software programmes and third-party systems, including CRM programmes, e-commerce platforms, logistics systems, and more. With the elimination of data silos, increased data accuracy, and seamless information exchange between systems, overall business efficiency is increased.
18. Better Financial Management: Accounting, budgeting, financial reporting, and cash management modules are all part of the comprehensive financial management capabilities offered by ERP systems. ERP systems allow businesses to efficiently manage their financial resources, keep track of spending, and improve financial planning by automating financial operations and supplying reliable financial data.
19. Enhanced Project Management: Project management modules are frequently included in ERP systems, which assist organisations in more efficient project planning, execution, and monitoring. These modules offer resources for task management, scheduling, resource allocation, and milestone monitoring, ensuring that projects are completed on schedule and within budget.

It is significant to remember that the benefits of ERP might vary based on the specific system, organisation size, sector, and implementation strategy.

Disadvantages of ERP

Although ERP have many benefits, there are also certain drawbacks that businesses need to be aware of. Making educated decisions concerning the implementation and management of ERP requires an understanding of these disadvantages. This section will examine the potential drawbacks of ERP and the difficulties that businesses may have when implementing and utilising these systems. It is crucial to keep in mind that the drawbacks might change based on a number of variables, including system complexity, deployment strategy, organisational readiness, and industry-specific requirements.

It's necessary to take into account the following issues when evaluating ERP's drawbacks:

1. ERP implementation might require a large commitment of money, time, and resources due to its complexity and expense. Employee training, data migration, initial setup, and customisation can be time-consuming and expensive. It may be difficult for small and medium-sized firms in particular to cover the upfront expenses related to ERP deployment.
2. Challenges with customization: ERP are made to accommodate a variety of industries and company procedures. Organisations, however, frequently have particular needs that can need tailoring the ERP software. Customization can be difficult, expensive, and time-consuming. Additionally, personalization may cause problems with compatibility when a system is upgraded or maintained.
3. User Resistance and Training: Changing existing workflows and processes in order to implement a new ERP frequently

results in employee resistance. There may be a temporary drop in productivity during the transition phase as a result of the need for additional training and support when adjusting to new software and practises.

4. ERP is feature-rich and comprehensive, which can make it difficult to understand and navigate. There may be a learning curve for users as they get used to the system's capabilities and functionality. The adoption and successful application of the ERP may be hampered by its complexity.
5. Integration difficulties: It might be difficult to integrate legacy systems and third-party applications with ERP. It may be necessary to spend more time and effort integrating because of compatibility problems, data mapping, and system interoperability. The system's capacity to offer a seamless flow of information throughout the organisation may be constrained by integration issues.
6. Risks Associated with Data Security and Privacy: ERP handle a sizable quantity of sensitive and important data, including as financial data, customer information, and intellectual property. ERP databases are vulnerable to security vulnerabilities due to their centralised structure. To guard against unauthorised access and data breaches, organisations must establish strong security measures including encryption, access limits, and frequent security audits.
7. Dependency on Vendors and Support: For continuing assistance, system updates, and bug patches, organisations depend on ERP vendors. The ERP maintenance and update process may become difficult if the vendor provides insufficient or timely support or goes out of business. Before choosing an ERP solution, businesses must carefully

consider the vendor's standing, financial standing, and long-term support obligations.
8. Potential Business Disruption: The deployment of an ERP system necessitates substantial system and process modifications. The switch to ERP can disrupt regular operations and short-term productivity loss if it is not managed well. To reduce disturbance during implementation, effective planning, change management, and communication are crucial.
9. Overemphasis on Technology: Because ERP is technology-driven solutions, organisations can focus too much on the technology side of things rather than taking into account the underlying organisational demands and business processes. This may lead to ineffective processes, a failure to align with corporate goals, and a failure to fully use system capabilities.
10. Lack of adaptability: ERP is made to offer a standardised approach to business processes. The flexibility of organisations to adjust to particular business requirements or changing market conditions, however, may be hampered by this standardisation. It can be necessary to make customizations, which can be expensive and interfere with the system's ability to accept future updates.
11. Upgrading and Maintenance: Regular upgrades and maintenance are necessary to keep ERP current. Upgrades may include difficult migration procedures and necessitate downtime, which may have an effect on business operations. The cost and time involved in system upgrades and continuous maintenance must be budgeted for by organisations.
12. Dependence on System Reliability: The ERP's dependability and stability become crucial for organisations. Technical problems or system outages can disrupt business operations

and reduce productivity. To lessen the effects of system failures, it is essential to have backup plans and mechanisms in place.

13. Rigidity and Resistance to Change: ERP frequently have established workflows and processes, which may not precisely correspond with a company's particular needs or changing commercial demands. It can be difficult and may require substantial customisation to update or add new functionality to the system, which increases complexity and expense.

14. Time and Resource Restraints: The organisation must devote a significant amount of time and resources to the implementation of ERP. Internal teams may feel the strain, and other projects or initiatives may be affected. To ensure the successful adoption and continued management of the ERP, organisations must properly plan and allot necessary resources.

15. ERP implementation frequently necessitates modifications to the organisational structure, roles, and duties. Employee resistance to change or ineffective change management techniques may prevent the system from being adopted and used successfully. For organisations to overcome resistance and guarantee user acceptability, effective change management practises must be invested in.

16. Challenges with data migration: Data migration from current systems to the new ERP can be difficult and time-consuming. To maintain data correctness and integrity, cleansing, mapping, and validation processes are required. Data loss, consistency issues, or delays in system installation can all be caused by data migration problems.

17. Specifically in organisations with multiple geographic locations or departments with different work cultures,

cultural hurdles may arise during ERP installation. User acceptance and system utilisation may be impacted by varied skill levels, language difficulties, and opposition to new technology. To effectively address these hurdles, adequate training and communication techniques are required.
18. Overemphasis on capabilities: Organisations may place too much emphasis on the ERP's capabilities at the expense of usability and user experience. Lack of user friendliness or intuitiveness can result in frustrated users, low adoption rates, and decreased productivity. Usability ought to be a top priority while choosing and implementing ERP.

It is crucial to remember that not all organisations may encounter these drawbacks, and the severity of each drawback may differ based on the particular ERP, organisation size, sector, and deployment strategy. Before making decisions on the deployment of ERP, it is crucial to evaluate these potential drawbacks in the context of the specific organisation and its particular requirements.

Applicability of ERP

The usefulness and relevance of ERP in various types of organisations and industries are referred to as its applicability. Although ERP have many features and benefits, their applicability can change depending on a number of situations. Consider the following important factors when determining whether ERP is appropriate:

1. Industry-specific Needs: ERP is made to meet the requirements of a variety of industries, including manufacturing, retail, healthcare, finance, and more. ERP's suitability for a certain sector is based on how well the system takes into account the unique needs and procedures of that

business. When installing an ERP, specific legislation, compliance requirements, or operational challenges may apply to some industries.
2. Organisational Size: ERP is applicable to businesses of all sizes, including small, medium-sized, and large firms. However, depending on the size of the organisation, the complexity and scope of the ERP system may vary. While larger businesses may need more powerful and customised systems to satisfy their broad needs, smaller organisations may choose to use simplified or scaled-down versions of ERP.
3. Business Processes and Complexity: The complexity and diversity of an organization's business processes determine the applicability of ERP. Organisations with numerous departments and activities that need to integrate and optimise their operations can benefit greatly from ERP. The potential for ERP to increase efficiency and coordination across various parts of the organisation increases with the complexity of the business operations.
4. Potential for Scalability and Growth: ERP should be able to support an organization's ambitions for future expansion. It is crucial to think about if the ERP solution can handle expansions in the future, extra users, higher transaction volumes, and changing company requirements. As businesses expand and flourish, they may continue to take advantage of ERP's advantages thanks to a scalable ERP.
5. Organisational Readiness: The ability of an organisation to absorb and embrace the changes that come with an ERP is a key factor in its successful adoption and use. Assessing aspects such the organization's culture, change management capabilities, IT infrastructure, and availability of experienced individuals is necessary for applicability. Organisations need

to be ready to put time, money, and effort into training staff, streamlining procedures, and adjusting to new working practises.

6. Cost Factors: The costs involved in implementing and maintaining the system have an impact on the applicability of ERP. An ERP can range widely in price when it comes to purchasing, implementing, customising, and maintaining it. Smaller businesses with tighter finances might need to carefully consider the ROI and determine whether the advantages outweigh the drawbacks.

7. Integration with Existing Systems: Businesses that already use software applications and other systems should assess how well ERP fits into and can be integrated with their existing setup. Smooth data flow is guaranteed via seamless integration, which also removes the need for double data entry or manual reconciliation.

8. Geographical Considerations: An organization's geographic distribution can have an impact on the application of ERP. ERP that supports multi-site administration, multi-language capabilities, and complies with foreign legislation may be needed by businesses with numerous sites or who conduct business internationally.

9. Customization and Flexibility: The applicability of ERP may depend on the level of customization and flexibility offered by the system. Some organizations may have unique or specialized processes that require tailored ERP solutions. Evaluating the customization options and flexibility of the ERP can help determine its applicability to specific organizational needs.

10. IT Infrastructure and Support: The organization's current IT infrastructure and technical support capabilities play a role in the application of ERP. To ensure that the ERP is

implemented, integrated, and maintained properly, it is vital to have sufficient hardware, network infrastructure, and IT assistance.

11. Vendor Choice and Industry experience: The ERP's applicability may be impacted by the vendor's choice and industry experience. To guarantee successful deployment and long-term maintenance, it is essential to choose a vendor with a track record of success, industry expertise, and a robust support structure.

12. Organisational Complexity: The degree of organisational complexity, which includes the quantity of divisions, affiliates, or business units, can affect the suitability of ERP. Businesses with decentralised operations or a variety of business units may need an ERP system that can handle intricate hierarchies and dependencies.

13. Regulation Compliance Needs: Sectors with strict regulatory compliance standards, such the healthcare, financial, or public sectors, require ERP that can handle these particular compliance requirements. The ability to maintain data security, privacy, and compliance with industry rules is directly related to the applicability of ERP in such industries.

14. Vendor and Ecosystem Compatibility: Businesses may take into account how well the ERP integrates with other programmes, devices, or platforms in their technological ecosystem. The entire usability and efficiency of the ERP can be impacted by integration abilities, APIs, and interoperability with third-party solutions.

It's vital to remember that the suitability of ERP will depend on the unique requirements, goals, and circumstances of each organisation. The optimal fit and applicability of an ERP for a given organisation can be ascertained by carrying out a thorough investigation, including stakeholders, and obtaining professional assistance.

2

Overview of Enterprise

In this chapter, we delve into enterprises, exploring their definition, types, and challenges. We also analyze how ERP benefits businesses, including the use of management information systems and business modeling. Through this exploration, our understanding of how businesses interact with ERP systems expands, enriching our knowledge in the process.

Introduction

In the context of ERP, an enterprise is a business organization engaged in commercial activities. It encompasses various sizes and industries, and its management involves multiple departments and processes. ERP systems streamline operations by integrating and automating business processes across functions like finance, HR, and supply chain. With a centralized database and interconnected modules, ERP facilitates seamless information flow, enhancing communication and decision-making. It caters to activities such as procurement, inventory management, sales, and finance, optimizing processes and providing real-time visibility. ERP systems offer industry-specific functionalities to address the unique needs of enterprises in different sectors.

In the context of ERP "Overview of Enterprise" refers to a comprehensive examination of enterprises from the perspective of how ERP systems can benefit and support their operations. It involves understanding the nature of enterprises, their various types, and the challenges they face in today's business environment. The overview also explores the specific advantages and functionalities of ERP that can address the unique needs and requirements of enterprises.

The overview delves into topics such as the integration of management information systems, which enables seamless data flow and collaboration across different departments and functions within an enterprise. It also covers the concept of modeling business processes with information systems, emphasizing how ERP can streamline and optimize operations.

This chapter highlights the importance of the Integrated Data Model (IDM) within ERP, ensuring data consistency and accuracy throughout the enterprise. It showcases how ERP systems can provide a centralized and reliable source of information for effective decision-making and improved overall performance.

The overview discusses the objectives and types of ERP systems, illustrating how enterprises can align their ERP implementation strategies with their specific goals and objectives. It provides insights into the functionalities and capabilities that different ERP systems offer, allowing enterprises to choose the most suitable solution for their needs.

Definition of Enterprise

A business organisation or firm that engages in commercial activities is referred to as an enterprise. It includes organisations of diverse sizes and works in a variety of industries, including both major multinational businesses and small and medium-sized enterprises (SMEs).

According to Cambridge Dictionary, enterprise is an organization, especially a business, or a difficult and important plan, especially one that will earn money.

Oxford Dictionary defines enterprise as the ability to think of new projects and make them successful or its the development of businesses by the people of a country rather than by the government.

The term "enterprise" has been used for centuries to describe a business organization or commercial endeavor. Its origin can be traced back to the Old French word "enterprenedre," which means "to undertake" or "to embark upon." This word was derived from the Latin word "interprendere," which carries a similar meaning of "to undertake" or "to take in hand."

Over time, the term "enterprise" evolved to encompass the idea of a venture or undertaking involving economic activities. It became a widely used term to refer to a business entity, encompassing all types of organizations, from small-scale enterprises to large corporations.

The concept of an enterprise has expanded beyond just the notion of a company or organization. It now represents a dynamic and multifaceted entity that encompasses various aspects such as entrepreneurship, innovation, risk-taking, and economic activity.

An enterprise represents a company or organization engaged in commercial activities, irrespective of its size or industry. It encompasses entities ranging from small and medium-sized enterprises (SMEs) to large multinational corporations.

When viewed through the lens of ERP, the definition of an enterprise goes beyond just its conventional understanding. It highlights the complex nature of an organization, including its various departments, functions, and processes that need to be efficiently managed and coordinated.

ERP systems are designed to support and optimize the operations of an enterprise by integrating and automating its diverse business processes. These processes can include procurement, inventory management, production planning, sales order processing, financial management, human resources, and more. ERP software provides a centralized database and interconnected modules that span different functional areas, enabling seamless flow of information and data across the organization.

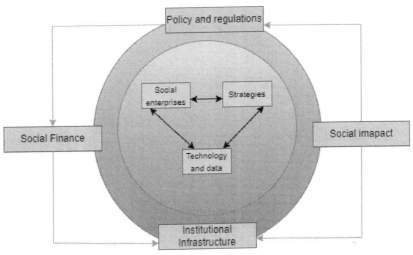

Figure 2. Components of a social entrepreneurship ecosystem

Types of enterprises

Types of enterprises can vary based on various factors, including their size, ownership structure, industry, and legal status. Understanding the different types of enterprises is important as it helps to classify and categorize businesses based on their characteristics and operating models. Here are some common types of enterprises:

1. Small and Medium-Sized Enterprises (SMEs): SMEs are businesses that have a relatively small number of employees and typically operate on a smaller scale compared to large corporations. They play a significant role in the economy, contributing to job creation and innovation.
2. Large Corporations: Large corporations are often multinational companies that have a significant presence in multiple countries. They typically have a large number of employees and extensive resources, allowing them to operate on a global scale.
3. Startups: Startups are newly established businesses that are in the early stages of their development. They are characterized by their innovative ideas, high-growth potential, and the pursuit of disruptive business models.
4. Family-Owned Businesses: Family-owned businesses are enterprises that are owned and operated by members of a single family. They often have a long-term perspective and may prioritize family values and continuity.
5. Non-Profit Organizations: Non-profit organizations are enterprises that operate for the benefit of society or specific causes rather than for making a profit. They are typically driven by a mission to address social, environmental, or cultural issues.
6. Public Sector Enterprises: Public sector enterprises are businesses that are owned and operated by the government. They serve various purposes, such as providing essential public services, promoting economic development, or managing natural resources.
7. Cooperative Enterprises: Cooperative enterprises are businesses that are owned and democratically controlled by the people who use their services or work in them. They

operate based on principles of cooperation, mutual benefit, and shared decision-making.

The category of legal forms or ownership structures of enterprises refers to the various ways in which businesses can be legally organized and owned. These forms determine the ownership rights, liabilities, decision-making authority, and legal obligations of the individuals or entities involved in the business. Some common categories of legal forms or ownership structures include:

1. Sole Proprietorship: Sole proprietorship is a type of enterprise where a single individual owns and operates the business. The owner has complete control over the business and assumes all the risks and responsibilities. It is the simplest form of business ownership and is often found in small-scale businesses or self-employed individuals.
2. Partnership: Partnership refers to a business structure where two or more individuals (partners) come together to jointly own and operate a business. Partnerships can be general partnerships, where all partners share equal responsibilities and liabilities, or limited partnerships, where there are both general partners and limited partners with different roles and liabilities.
3. Private Limited Companies: Private Limited Companies, often denoted as "Pvt. Ltd.", are privately held businesses owned by shareholders. These companies have a separate legal identity from their owners and offer limited liability protection to their shareholders. Private limited companies are typically smaller in scale and have restrictions on the transferability of shares.
4. Public Limited Companies: Public Limited Companies, often denoted as "PLC" or "Limited (Ltd.)", are publicly traded companies whose shares are available for purchase by

the general public through stock exchanges. These companies have a wider ownership base and are subject to additional regulatory requirements. Public limited companies often have a larger scale of operations and can raise capital by issuing shares to the public.

Challenges facing enterprises

In today's dynamic business environment, enterprises face a multitude of challenges that can impact their operations, growth, and sustainability. These challenges arise from various sources, both internal and external, and require careful management and strategic decision-making. Let's delve into some of the key challenges facing enterprises:

1. Technological Advancements: Rapid technological advancements present both opportunities and challenges for enterprises. Keeping up with evolving technologies and digital transformation is crucial for businesses to remain competitive. However, the pace of technological change can be overwhelming, requiring continuous investment in technology infrastructure, cybersecurity measures, and workforce upskilling.
2. Globalization and International Competition: Globalization has opened doors to new markets and opportunities, but it has also intensified competition. Enterprises must navigate complex global supply chains, cultural differences, and market fluctuations. Developing strategies to enter new markets, manage international operations, and differentiate themselves in a global marketplace are essential for sustained success.
3. Economic Uncertainty: Economic fluctuations, recessions, and financial crises pose significant challenges for

enterprises. Uncertainty in the global economy can affect consumer demand, market conditions, and financial stability. Enterprises must be adaptable and agile to navigate through economic downturns, manage costs, and identify new growth opportunities.

4. Changing Customer Expectations: Customer expectations are continuously evolving, driven by technological advancements, increased connectivity, and personalized experiences. Enterprises must understand and respond to changing customer preferences, enhance their customer experience strategies, and provide products and services that meet the evolving needs and desires of their target market.

5. Talent Acquisition and Retention: Finding and retaining skilled and talented employees is a persistent challenge for enterprises. The demand for specialized skills, such as data analytics, artificial intelligence, and cybersecurity, is high. Enterprises must develop effective talent acquisition and retention strategies, foster a positive work culture, and invest in employee development to attract and retain top talent.

6. Regulatory and Compliance Requirements: Enterprises operate within a complex web of regulatory frameworks and compliance requirements. Adhering to laws and regulations related to finance, data privacy, employment, and industry-specific standards is critical. Ensuring compliance can be challenging due to the evolving nature of regulations and the need for robust internal controls and risk management processes.

7. Innovation and Disruption: Enterprises must continuously innovate and adapt to stay ahead of disruptive forces. Technological advancements, changing consumer preferences, and new market entrants can disrupt established business models and industries. Embracing

innovation, fostering a culture of creativity, and investing in research and development are essential to thrive in a rapidly changing business landscape.

8. Environmental Sustainability: Environmental concerns and sustainability have become significant challenges for enterprises. Businesses are increasingly expected to operate in an environmentally responsible manner, reduce their carbon footprint, and adopt sustainable practices throughout their value chain. Developing sustainable strategies, implementing green initiatives, and aligning with environmental regulations are essential considerations for enterprises.

9. Risk Management: Enterprises face a wide range of risks, including operational, financial, reputational, and cybersecurity risks. Managing these risks requires robust risk management frameworks, proactive monitoring, and mitigation strategies. Enterprises must identify potential risks, develop contingency plans, and implement measures to protect their assets, reputation, and stakeholders' interests.

10. Changing Business Models: The rapid pace of technological advancements and market disruptions necessitate continuous adaptation of business models. Enterprises must be willing to embrace new business models, explore innovative revenue streams, and be open to collaboration and partnerships to stay relevant and competitive.

Successfully navigating these challenges requires strategic planning, effective leadership, agility, and a proactive approach to change. Enterprises that can anticipate and adapt to these challenges are better positioned to seize opportunities, drive growth, and thrive in an ever-evolving business landscape.

Need of ERP for enterprises

The need for Enterprise Resource Planning (ERP) systems in enterprises is driven by various factors that contribute to their growth, efficiency, and competitiveness in today's dynamic business environment. ERP serves as a comprehensive solution that integrates and streamlines diverse business processes, enabling organizations to achieve operational excellence and strategic objectives. Let's dig into into the key points highlighting the need for ERP in enterprises:

1. Streamlined Operations: ERP systems provide a centralized platform that connects different functional areas within an enterprise, such as finance, human resources, supply chain, manufacturing, sales, and customer relationship management. By integrating these processes, ERP eliminates data silos and manual workflows, promoting seamless information flow and collaboration. This streamlines operations, reduces duplication of efforts, and enhances overall efficiency.
2. Improved Decision-Making: ERP systems offer real-time and accurate data visibility across the organization. This enables informed decision-making at various levels, from operational to strategic. Decision-makers can access key performance indicators, reports, and analytics, empowering them to make data-driven decisions promptly. With comprehensive insights into financials, inventory levels, production schedules, and customer trends, enterprises can adapt quickly to market changes and gain a competitive edge.
3. Enhanced Productivity: ERP automates routine tasks and workflows, minimizing manual data entry and paperwork. This frees up employee time, allowing them to focus on more

value-added activities. Additionally, ERP eliminates redundant processes, reduces errors, and improves data accuracy, leading to increased productivity across the organization. Employees can leverage ERP's user-friendly interfaces and self-service capabilities to access information, collaborate, and perform tasks efficiently.

4. Scalability and Flexibility: As enterprises grow and evolve, their systems and processes need to adapt. ERP systems offer scalability and flexibility to accommodate changing business requirements. They can handle increased transaction volumes, support multi-site operations, and integrate with external systems. This scalability allows enterprises to expand their operations, enter new markets, and pursue strategic initiatives without technological constraints.

5. Data Integration and Reporting: ERP acts as a centralized data repository, ensuring data consistency and integrity across the organization. It eliminates data duplication and provides a single source of truth for reporting and analysis. Enterprises can generate comprehensive reports, dashboards, and analytics to gain insights into key metrics and performance indicators. This empowers management to monitor operations, track progress, identify trends, and make data-backed decisions.

6. Regulatory Compliance: Enterprises must adhere to various industry regulations and compliance standards. ERP systems offer built-in controls and features that help organizations meet regulatory requirements. They facilitate accurate financial reporting, data security, and audit trails, ensuring compliance with legal and industry-specific regulations. This minimizes the risk of non-compliance penalties and reputational damage.

7. **Customer Satisfaction and Retention:** ERP systems enable enterprises to improve customer satisfaction and retention by providing better visibility into customer interactions, order management, and service delivery. With real-time data, enterprises can respond promptly to customer inquiries, track orders, and provide accurate delivery information. This enhances the customer experience, builds trust, and fosters long-term relationships.

8. **Business Intelligence and Innovation:** ERP systems incorporate business intelligence tools and analytics capabilities, allowing enterprises to gain insights into market trends, customer behavior, and operational performance. These insights drive innovation, enabling enterprises to identify new business opportunities, optimize processes, and develop competitive strategies. ERP acts as a foundation for digital transformation initiatives, facilitating the adoption of emerging technologies such as artificial intelligence, machine learning, and Internet of Things (IoT).

By implementing an ERP system tailored to their specific needs, enterprises can effectively navigate the complexities of modern business and position themselves.

Integration of Management Information System

The integration of the Management Information System (MIS) is a key component of ERP systems. It plays a crucial role in enabling seamless information flow and collaboration across different departments and functions within an enterprise. The integration of MIS within ERP ensures that relevant data is shared and accessible throughout the organization, promoting efficient decision-making and effective management.

A MIS is a computer-based system that collects, processes, stores, and disseminates information to support managerial decision-making within an organization. It is a framework of interconnected components, including hardware, software, databases, and people, working together to manage and distribute information within the organization.

The primary purpose of an MIS is to provide relevant and timely information to managers at all levels of the organization, enabling them to make informed decisions and take appropriate actions. It captures data from various sources, processes it into meaningful information, and presents it in a structured format for analysis and decision-making.

The components of an MIS typically include:

1. Data Collection: The MIS collects data from different sources, such as internal systems, external databases, and manual inputs. This data can include financial information, sales data, inventory levels, employee records, customer information, and more.
2. Data Processing: The collected data is processed and transformed into useful information through various operations, such as sorting, filtering, aggregating, calculating, and summarizing. This processing ensures that the data is organized and presented in a meaningful and understandable way.
3. Data Storage: The processed information is stored in databases or data warehouses, where it can be accessed and retrieved as needed. The storage systems provide a secure and centralized repository for the data, ensuring data integrity and availability.
4. Information Retrieval: The MIS allows users to retrieve and access the stored information based on their specific needs.

This retrieval can be done through queries, reports, dashboards, or customized interfaces, providing users with the flexibility to access the information in a way that suits their requirements.

5. Information Presentation: The MIS presents the information in a structured and visually appealing format, such as tables, charts, graphs, and reports. This presentation makes the information easier to understand and interpret, facilitating effective decision-making.
6. Decision Support: The MIS provides decision support capabilities by offering tools and functionalities for analysis, forecasting, modeling, and simulation. These features assist managers in evaluating different scenarios, assessing risks, and making informed decisions based on the available information.

The role of an MIS is to support managerial functions, including planning, organizing, controlling, and decision-making. It helps managers monitor performance, analyze trends, identify problems and opportunities, allocate resources, and evaluate outcomes.

A MIS is a vital component of organizational management, enabling efficient information management, effective decision-making, and improved performance within an organization.

In an ERP system, the integration of MIS involves the consolidation and synchronization of data from various sources and functional areas, such as finance, human resources, supply chain, manufacturing, sales, and customer relationship management. The MIS component of ERP captures, stores, processes, and presents data in a structured and meaningful way.

By integrating MIS within ERP, enterprises can achieve the following benefits:

1. Data Consistency: Integration ensures that data remains consistent across all functional areas within the organization. Any updates or changes made to data in one module of the ERP system automatically propagate to other relevant modules, eliminating data discrepancies and ensuring accuracy.
2. Real-time Information: MIS integration provides real-time access to information, enabling stakeholders to make timely and informed decisions. Data is updated in real-time, reflecting the latest transactions and activities within the organization. This promotes agility and responsiveness in managing operations.
3. Streamlined Workflows: MIS integration facilitates the automation and streamlining of workflows. It eliminates manual data entry and repetitive tasks, reducing errors and improving operational efficiency. With integrated MIS, information flows seamlessly between different modules, enabling smooth business processes and reducing time and effort required for data synchronization.
4. Enhanced Collaboration: The integration of MIS promotes collaboration among different departments and teams within an enterprise. Relevant data and information are readily available to authorized users, fostering effective communication and collaboration across the organization. This improves cross-functional coordination and facilitates better decision-making.
5. Comprehensive Reporting and Analysis: The integration of MIS enables enterprises to generate comprehensive reports and perform in-depth analysis. Data from different functional areas can be combined and analyzed to gain insights into business performance, identify trends, and support strategic decision-making. MIS integration provides

a holistic view of the organization's operations, allowing stakeholders to evaluate performance and take appropriate actions.
6. Efficient Resource Utilization: By integrating MIS within ERP, enterprises can optimize resource allocation and utilization. They can track and manage resources, such as personnel, inventory, and equipment, more effectively. This leads to better resource planning, improved operational efficiency, and cost savings.

The integration of MIS within ERP ensures that the right information is available to the right people at the right time. It enables enterprises to streamline workflows, improve collaboration, enhance decision-making, and optimize resource utilization. This integration is essential for maximizing the benefits of ERP systems and achieving operational excellence within the organization.

Modelling Business with Information Systems

Business modeling is a process that involves creating a simplified representation of a business, including its activities, processes, and resources. The goal is to gain a deeper understanding of the business and support decision-making. By visually depicting the business's components and their relationships, organizations can effectively communicate complex concepts, identify inefficiencies, and explore opportunities for improvement.

Business modeling provides a framework for analyzing different scenarios and strategies. Organizations can simulate the impact of potential changes, such as process redesign or technology implementation, to assess risks and benefits. This enables data-driven decision-making based on projected outcomes.

Aligning operations with strategic objectives and industry best practices is another benefit of business modeling. By mapping processes to standardized models or frameworks, organizations can identify gaps, redundancies, and areas for improvement. This streamlines operations, enhances efficiency, and ensures compliance with regulations and industry standards.

Various techniques and tools, such as process mapping, data modeling, and workflow diagrams, can be used for business modeling. Collaboration with stakeholders at different levels of the organization is often necessary to create a comprehensive representation.

"Modelling Business with Information Systems" involves the use of information systems to represent and analyze various aspects of a business in a structured and systematic manner. It is a process that combines business knowledge, technology, and data modeling techniques to create a virtual representation of the organization's activities, processes, and resources.

Through business modeling, organizations can gain a deeper understanding of their operations, identify areas for improvement, and make informed decisions based on data-driven insights. Information systems provide the tools and frameworks to capture and represent the complex relationships between different elements of the business, such as processes, departments, functions, and resources.

Business modeling enables organizations to visualize and simulate different scenarios, allowing them to assess the impact of potential changes, strategies, or investments. By creating models that reflect the current state of the business and its desired future state, organizations can identify gaps, inefficiencies, or bottlenecks, and develop strategies to optimize their operations.

Information systems play a crucial role in facilitating business modeling by providing the necessary tools and functionalities. These systems allow organizations to capture and store relevant data, define relationships between different entities, and generate visual representations such as diagrams, flowcharts, or process maps.

Information systems support the integration of data from various sources, enabling organizations to create a comprehensive and holistic view of their business. By combining data from different systems and departments, organizations can analyze the interdependencies between different processes, identify potential risks or dependencies, and design solutions that enhance efficiency and effectiveness.

Business modeling with information systems also enables organizations to align their business processes with industry best practices or specific standards. By mapping their processes to standardized models or frameworks, organizations can identify areas of non-compliance or opportunities for optimization, ensuring that their operations are in line with industry norms or regulatory requirements.

Information systems support the continuous improvement and evolution of business models. As organizations adapt to changing market dynamics, customer demands, or internal factors, they can update their models to reflect the new realities and align their operations accordingly. Information systems provide the flexibility and agility to modify and enhance models as needed, allowing organizations to remain competitive and responsive in a rapidly evolving business environment.

Modeling business with information systems is a powerful approach for organizations to gain insights into their operations, optimize processes, and make informed decisions. By leveraging the capabilities of information systems, organizations can create virtual representations of their business, analyze complex relationships, and drive continuous improvement.

The Integrated Data Model (IDM)

Standardizing data elements, relationships, and attributes is crucial in the context of the Integrated Data Model (IDM) within ERP system. This standardization process ensures that data is organized and structured in a consistent manner, allowing for seamless integration of data from various sources. By establishing a uniform format and structure, the IDM enables efficient data flow and eliminates data inconsistencies or discrepancies that can arise from disparate data sources.

One of the primary functions of the IDM is to facilitate the smooth flow of data across different modules and departments within an organization. By eliminating the need for duplicate data entry and ensuring the availability of accurate information in real-time, the IDM significantly improves operational efficiency. Employees can access up-to-date data from a centralized source, enabling them to make informed decisions and carry out their tasks more effectively.

In addition to data flow optimization, the IDM plays a critical role in centralizing data storage, management, and access. It establishes a robust data governance framework that includes security measures, access controls, and compliance mechanisms. By implementing data governance policies and procedures, organizations can maintain data integrity, protect sensitive information, and adhere to regulatory requirements.

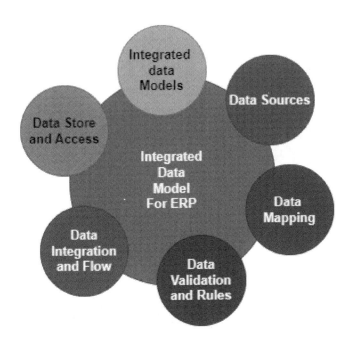

Figure 3. Integrated Data Model (IDM) from ERP

Fig. 3 shows the integration of an IDM within ERP system. The IDM serves as a central component that manages and integrates data from various sources. Data sources provide input data, which is then mapped and validated using data mapping and data validation components. The data integration and flow processes ensure seamless integration of data across different modules and functionalities within the ERP. Finally, the data store and access component ensures efficient storage and retrieval of data within the IDM.

The IDM enables the integration of data from different functional areas and business processes, offering organizations a holistic view of their operations. This comprehensive integration facilitates data-driven decision-making by providing decision-makers with accurate and timely information. The IDM supports analytics and reporting functionalities, allowing organizations to generate meaningful insights, identify trends, and identify areas for improvement.

Data consistency and accuracy are paramount within the IDM. By enforcing validation rules, data integrity checks, and data quality control measures, the IDM helps ensure the reliability of information. It reduces the risk of errors, inconsistencies, and redundant data, providing users with trustworthy and consistent data for decision-making purposes.

The IDM serves as a consolidated and reliable data source for reporting and analytics. Organizations can perform data analysis, generate reports, and extract valuable insights from the IDM. This enables them to identify patterns, trends, and opportunities for business growth and optimization.

The specific structure and implementation of the IDM can be customized to meet the unique requirements of each organization and the ERP system in use. Organizations can tailor the IDM to align with their specific business needs, processes, and industry requirements. This flexibility allows for seamless integration with existing systems and ensures that the IDM serves as an effective tool for data management and optimization.

Implementing an IDM brings several benefits to organizations. Improved operational efficiency, streamlined processes, enhanced data governance, better decision-making, and overall organizational effectiveness are some of the key advantages. The IDM empowers organizations to leverage data as a strategic asset, enabling them to make informed decisions, gain a competitive edge, and drive growth and success in today's data-centric business landscape.

Objectives of ERP

The objectives of an ERP system are multifaceted and encompass various aspects of business operations. ERP aims to integrate different functions and departments within an organization, centralizing data and information across areas such as finance, human resources, supply chain management, manufacturing, sales, and customer relationship management. This integration facilitates cross-functional collaboration and provides a unified view of the organization.

Another objective of ERP is to streamline and optimize business processes. By automating repetitive tasks and standardizing workflows, ERP enhances operational efficiency, reduces errors, and accelerates the speed of business operations. This objective ensures consistent and standardized processes across the organization, leading to improved productivity and cost savings.

Data visibility and accuracy are key objectives of ERP. By centralizing data in a single database, ERP eliminates data duplication and inconsistencies. This objective enables stakeholders to access up-to-date information, make informed decisions, and respond quickly to changing business needs. Accurate data improves forecasting, planning, and overall business performance.

ERP systems also aim to provide robust reporting and analytics capabilities. Customizable dashboards, key performance indicators (KPIs), and analytics tools enable organizations to monitor and measure business performance. ERP supports data-driven decision-making, enabling organizations to generate comprehensive reports, perform in-depth data analysis, and gain insights into various aspects of their operations.

Customer relationship management (CRM) is another objective of ERP. By integrating customer data, sales processes, and customer support functions, ERP enables organizations to deliver personalized customer experiences, track customer interactions, manage sales pipelines, and provide efficient after-sales service. This objective helps organizations build strong customer relationships, increase customer loyalty, and drive business growth.

Scalability and flexibility are important objectives of ERP systems. They are designed to accommodate organizational growth and changing business requirements. ERP provides a platform that can scale up or down as per the organization's needs, support new functionalities, and easily integrate with other software applications. This scalability and flexibility ensure that the ERP system can evolve alongside the organization, supporting its long-term growth and competitiveness.

Addressing regulatory compliance is another objective of ERP. ERP systems include features and controls to ensure adherence to industry standards, government regulations, and financial reporting guidelines. By enforcing compliance measures within the system, ERP helps organizations mitigate risks, maintain data integrity, and avoid legal and financial penalties.

Some additional objectives that organizations may seek to achieve through ERP implementation include:

Supply chain optimization is a key objective, as ERP helps streamline supply chain processes such as procurement, inventory management, and logistics. This optimization ensures timely product delivery and maximizes supply chain efficiency.

Cost reduction is another objective of ERP implementation. By identifying cost-saving opportunities, eliminating redundant processes, optimizing inventory levels, and improving resource allocation, ERP systems help organizations achieve greater operational efficiency and reduce expenses.

ERP also focuses on enhancing collaboration and communication within the organization. By providing a centralized platform for real-time information sharing, document collaboration, and updates, ERP fosters effective communication and collaboration among different departments, teams, and stakeholders.

Business intelligence is a critical objective of ERP systems. With built-in business intelligence tools, organizations can extract valuable insights from their data, perform data analysis, and gain a deeper understanding of their business performance and trends. This empowers decision-makers with the information they need to make informed strategic decisions.

Standardization and best practices are promoted by ERP systems. By adopting standardized processes and industry best practices, organizations ensure consistency, efficiency, and quality throughout their operations. This objective helps eliminate variations and inefficiencies, leading to improved performance and customer satisfaction.

Change management is often required during ERP implementation. Therefore, one objective of ERP is to effectively manage the change process. This involves ensuring smooth adoption, providing user training, and minimizing resistance to change. Effective change management ensures a successful ERP implementation and user acceptance.

ERP offers a competitive advantage to organizations. By enabling them to respond quickly to market changes, customer demands, and emerging opportunities, ERP supports efficient resource allocation and effective decision-making. This competitive edge helps organizations stay ahead in a dynamic business environment.

Types of ERP

ERP systems can be classified into different types based on specific criteria, helping organizations choose a solution that aligns with their needs and industry requirements. Understanding these types allows businesses to make informed decisions, optimize processes, and achieve greater efficiency and productivity. Each type offers unique features and benefits, supporting efficient operations and contributing to organizational success.

Types of ERP systems can be classified based on several factors, including deployment model, functionality, industry focus, and scalability. Here are some common classifications of ERP systems:

1. Deployment Model:

When it comes to ERP systems, one important aspect to consider is the deployment model. The deployment model refers to how the ERP software is implemented and hosted within an organization. It plays a crucial role in determining factors such as infrastructure requirements, accessibility, control, and maintenance.

    a. On-premises ERP: On-premises ERP refers to the deployment model where the ERP system is installed and operated on the organization's own servers and infrastructure. In this approach, the organization is responsible for managing the hardware, software, and IT infrastructure required to run the ERP system. This deployment model provides organizations with full control over their data and allows for customization and integration with existing systems. It also requires significant upfront investment and ongoing maintenance costs. On-premises ERP is suitable for organizations that prioritize data security, have specific customization requirements, and have the resources and IT capabilities to manage the system internally.

b. Cloud-based ERP: Cloud-based ERP refers to the deployment model where the ERP software is hosted and managed by a third-party provider, and organizations access the system over the internet. In this approach, the ERP system is hosted on remote servers, and organizations can access it through web browsers or dedicated applications. Cloud-based ERP offers advantages such as scalability, flexibility, and cost-effectiveness, as organizations can pay for the services they use and scale up or down as needed. It eliminates the need for on-premises infrastructure and reduces IT maintenance responsibilities. However, organizations must rely on the provider for data security, availability, and system performance. Cloud-based ERP is suitable for organizations seeking agility, rapid deployment, and the ability to access the system from anywhere, as long as there is an internet connection.

c. Hybrid ERP: Hybrid ERP is an approach that combines elements of both on-premises and cloud-based ERP deployments. It allows organizations to have a mix of cloud and on-premises systems based on their specific needs and requirements. With hybrid ERP, organizations can leverage the benefits of both deployment models. They can choose to keep certain sensitive data or critical functions on-premises for greater control and security while using cloud-based solutions for scalability, flexibility, and cost savings. Hybrid ERP offers organizations the flexibility to adapt their ERP environment based on changing business needs, allowing them to strike a balance between security, control, and the advantages of cloud technology.

2. Functionality:

When it comes to ERP systems, one important aspect to consider is the functionality they offer. ERP systems can be classified based on their functionality, which refers to the specific modules and features they provide to support various business processes. Understanding the different functionality types of ERP systems is crucial for organizations to ensure that the chosen solution aligns with their specific operational needs and industry requirements. The functionality of an ERP system plays a significant role in driving efficiency, improving productivity, and facilitating seamless integration across different departments.

   a. Core ERP: Core ERP systems are the foundation of an organization's ERP infrastructure, providing essential functionalities that are crucial for day-to-day operations. These systems typically include modules for finance, human resources, supply chain management, and manufacturing. Finance modules handle financial transactions, accounting, budgeting, and reporting. Human resources modules manage employee information, payroll, benefits, and workforce planning. Supply chain management modules oversee procurement, inventory management, and logistics. Manufacturing modules support production planning, scheduling, and quality control. Core ERP systems ensure that key business processes are efficiently managed, enabling organizations to streamline operations, enhance productivity, and make data-driven decisions.

b. Extended ERP: Extended ERP systems go beyond the core functionalities and provide additional modules and features tailored to specific industries or business processes. These systems may include customer relationship management (CRM) modules to manage customer interactions, sales, and marketing activities. Project management modules help organizations plan, execute, and track projects effectively. E-commerce modules enable online selling and integrate with other business processes. Extended ERP systems cater to the unique needs of different industries and provide comprehensive solutions to optimize operations, improve customer engagement, and drive business growth. By incorporating specialized modules, organizations can enhance their capabilities and align their ERP system with industry-specific requirements.

3. Industry Focus:

When it comes to ERP, industry focus plays a significant role in delivering tailored solutions to meet the specific needs of different sectors. ERP can be categorized based on industry focus, where each type is designed to address the unique challenges and requirements of a particular industry. This industry-specific approach allows organizations to benefit from ERP that are customized to their specific workflows, regulations, and best practices. By aligning the ERP with the intricacies of their industry, businesses can optimize their operations, improve efficiency, and gain a competitive edge. Whether it is manufacturing, healthcare, retail, or any other sector, industry-focused ERP enable organizations to leverage industry-specific functionalities and capabilities to streamline processes, enhance decision-making, and drive growth.

    a. Vertical ERP: Vertical ERP systems are designed to cater to the unique needs of a specific industry or vertical, offering specialized functionalities and features that align with the industry's requirements. Whether it is healthcare, manufacturing, retail, or banking, these ERP systems are tailored to address the industry-specific challenges, regulations, and best practices. By focusing on the specific needs of a particular industry, vertical ERP systems enable organizations to streamline their operations, enhance productivity, and improve decision-making within their industry context. These systems provide industry-specific modules, workflows, and reporting capabilities, allowing businesses to effectively manage their operations and gain a competitive advantage in their respective sectors.

    b. Horizontal ERP: Horizontal ERP are designed to be versatile and applicable across multiple industries. They offer a broad range of functionalities and can be customized to meet the specific needs of different businesses. These provide a foundation of core modules, such as finance, human resources, and supply chain management that are essential for any organization regardless of industry. They offer flexibility in terms of configuration and customization to align with specific business processes and requirements. Horizontal ERP allow businesses from various industries to benefit from standardized processes, integrated data management, and improved operational efficiency. They provide a scalable and adaptable solution that can support businesses as they grow and evolve, regardless of the industry they operate in.

4. Scalability:

Scalability is a crucial factor to consider when choosing an ERP system. The ability of an ERP solution to scale and adapt to changing business needs is essential for long-term success. Scalability refers to the system's capacity to handle increasing data volumes, users, and transactions without sacrificing performance or efficiency. An ERP system with robust scalability enables organizations to seamlessly accommodate business growth, whether it's expanding into new markets, acquiring additional business units, or increasing customer demand. By ensuring scalability, businesses can future-proof their ERP investment, minimize disruption during periods of growth, and maintain optimal system performance even as operational requirements evolve. The scalability of an ERP system plays a significant role in providing organizations with the flexibility and agility they need to stay competitive in today's dynamic business landscape.

    a. Small and Medium-sized Enterprises (SME) ERP: Small and Medium-sized Enterprises (SME) ERP systems cater to the specific needs of small and medium-sized businesses that have limited resources and scalability requirements. These ERP solutions are designed to be cost-effective, easy to implement, and scalable to accommodate the growth of SMEs. They offer essential functionalities such as finance, inventory management, sales, and customer relationship management, tailored to the specific needs of smaller organizations. SME ERP systems help streamline business processes, improve operational efficiency, and provide better visibility into key business metrics. They are a practical choice for SMEs looking to leverage ERP technology to enhance their competitiveness and drive business growth.

b. Enterprise ERP: Enterprise ERP systems are designed for larger organizations with complex operations and scalability needs. These systems are capable of handling a high volume of transactions, supporting multiple locations, and accommodating a large user base. Enterprise ERP solutions offer comprehensive functionalities that cover various aspects of business operations, including finance, supply chain management, human resources, manufacturing, and customer relationship management. They provide robust features for managing complex organizational structures, global operations, and multi-currency transactions. These ERP systems enable large enterprises to streamline processes, enhance collaboration, and gain insights into their operations for informed decision-making. They offer scalability and flexibility to meet the evolving needs of the organization as it grows and expands its operations.

5. Open-source ERP:

Open-source ERP refers to ERP software distributed under an open-source license, allowing organizations to access, modify, and distribute the source code freely. These solutions offer cost-effectiveness, customization flexibility, and the ability to integrate with other applications. With features supporting various business functions, open-source ERP fosters collaboration, innovation, and knowledge sharing. Organizations benefit from cost savings, customization options, and a supportive development community.

It's important to note that ERP systems can overlap across these classifications, and some systems may have characteristics from multiple categories. The classification of ERP types can help organizations narrow down their options and choose an ERP solution that aligns with their specific requirements and business objectives.

In this chapter we have provided an overview of enterprise, including its definition, types, and the challenges it faces. The need for ERP in enterprises was discussed, along with the integration of Management Information Systems and the concept of modeling business with information systems. The chapter introduced the Integrated Data Model (IDM) and outlined the objectives of ERP. It also covered the different types of ERP systems. In Chapter 3, we will delve into ERP from a manufacturing perspective, exploring its applications and benefits in the manufacturing industry.

3

ERP — A Manufacturing Perspective

In Chapter 2, we explored enterprises and their advantages with ERP for businesses. Now, in these section, our attention turns to ERP in manufacturing. This chapter will delve into different facets of ERP in manufacturing. Here, we'll examine specific applications of ERP in the manufacturing industry, delving deeper into its practical use.

Introduction to ERP in Manufacturing

In this chapter, we will explore the realm of ERP from a manufacturing perspective. Throughout this chapter, we will dive into various key concepts and practices that play a crucial role in the manufacturing industry. Topics such as Material Requirement Planning (MRP), Manufacturing Resource Planning-II (MRP-II), Distribution Requirement Planning (DRP), Just-In-Time (JIT) and Kanban System, Process Management, Work Management, Workflow Management, Work History Management, and Product Data Management (PDM) will be covered in detail. By understanding how ERP is applied in the manufacturing sector, we will gain valuable insights into how these systems optimize operations, streamline processes, and drive success in the industry.

Material Requirement Planning (MRP)

Material Requirement Planning (MRP) is a fundamental component of ERP systems, specifically designed to streamline and optimize the management of materials and inventory within the manufacturing process.

Understanding Material Requirement Planning:

Material Requirement Planning aims to ensure that the right materials are available at the right time and in the right quantities, minimizing stockouts, excess inventory, and production delays. It involves the systematic analysis and planning of material needs throughout the production cycle, encompassing both raw materials and components required for manufacturing operations.

Key Elements of Material Requirement Planning:

MRP relies on accurate inventory data, bill of materials (BOM), and production schedules to perform its functions effectively. The core elements of MRP include:

1. Bill of Materials (BOM): The BOM serves as a detailed list of all components, sub-assemblies, and raw materials required to produce a finished product. It forms the foundation of MRP calculations and assists in determining material requirements.
2. Master Production Schedule (MPS): The MPS outlines the production plan, specifying the quantity and timing of finished goods to be manufactured within a given timeframe. It acts as a crucial input for MRP calculations.
3. Inventory Management: MRP relies on accurate and up-to-date inventory data to calculate material requirements. Real-

time inventory monitoring, stock levels, and consumption rates are essential for successful MRP implementation.
4. Lead Time Analysis: Lead time analysis involves determining the time required to procure materials, process them, and incorporate them into the production cycle. Accurate lead time calculations ensure that materials are ordered and delivered in a timely manner, avoiding production delays.
5. MRP Calculations: Based on the BOM, MPS, inventory data, and lead time analysis, MRP software performs calculations to determine the optimal quantity and timing of material orders. It considers factors such as reorder points, safety stock levels, and dependent demand to generate accurate material requirement plans.

Benefits and Challenges of Material Requirement Planning:

Implementing an effective MRP system brings numerous benefits to manufacturing organizations. These include improved inventory control, reduced carrying costs, optimized production schedules, enhanced supply chain management, and increased customer satisfaction through timely deliveries. However, challenges such as data accuracy, system integration, and managing dynamic demand fluctuations need to be carefully addressed to reap the full benefits of MRP.

Implementation Considerations:

Successfully implementing MRP requires careful planning, collaboration between departments, and alignment with organizational goals. Key considerations include selecting the right MRP software, data management and accuracy, training and education for users, integration with other ERP modules, and continuous monitoring and refinement of the MRP system to adapt to changing business needs.

Material Requirement Planning plays a pivotal role in optimizing inventory management and streamlining production processes in the manufacturing industry. By accurately forecasting material requirements and synchronizing them with production schedules, MRP helps organizations achieve cost efficiency, reduce stockouts, and enhance overall operational performance. Understanding the principles and implementation considerations of MRP is crucial for organizations seeking to leverage ERP to their full potential in the realm of manufacturing.

Manufacturing Resource Planning-II (MRP-II)

Manufacturing Resource Planning-II (MRP-II) is an advanced extension of Material Requirement Planning (MRP). MRP-II expands the scope of traditional MRP systems by incorporating additional functionalities to optimize resources and streamline manufacturing operations. We explore the principles, features, and benefits of MRP-II, as well as its implementation considerations in the context of enterprise-wide resource planning.

Understanding Manufacturing Resource Planning-II:

Manufacturing Resource Planning-II, often referred to as MRP-II, builds upon the foundation of MRP to provide a comprehensive approach to resource planning in manufacturing organizations. MRP-II extends beyond material management to encompass other critical resources, such as labor, machinery, facilities, and financial resources. By integrating various aspects of production, MRP-II enables organizations to optimize resource allocation, improve production efficiency, and achieve greater control over their manufacturing operations.

Key Components of Manufacturing Resource Planning-II:

MRP-II incorporates several key components that contribute to its holistic resource planning capabilities:

1. Capacity Planning: MRP-II includes advanced capacity planning tools that help organizations analyze and manage their production capacities. It takes into account factors such as labor availability, machine capacity, and production constraints to ensure that resources are allocated efficiently and production schedules are realistic.
2. Shop Floor Control: MRP-II provides real-time visibility and control over shop floor activities, allowing organizations to monitor production progress, track work orders, manage work-in-progress, and facilitate efficient communication between different departments on the shop floor.
3. Cost Management: MRP-II incorporates cost management features, enabling organizations to track and analyze manufacturing costs at various levels, such as product, order, and operation. This facilitates cost control, cost estimation, and cost-based decision-making in manufacturing processes.
4. Financial Integration: MRP-II integrates financial data with production planning, enabling organizations to analyze the financial impact of manufacturing decisions and align production activities with financial objectives. It facilitates cost accounting, budgeting, and financial reporting in the manufacturing context.

Benefits and Challenges of Manufacturing Resource Planning-II:

Implementing MRP-II offers numerous benefits to manufacturing organizations. These include improved resource utilization, enhanced production planning and control, optimized scheduling, better demand forecasting, streamlined supply chain management, and increased overall operational efficiency. However, challenges such as data accuracy, system complexity, integration with other business functions, and change management need to be carefully addressed to ensure successful MRP-II implementation.

Implementation Considerations:

Implementing MRP-II requires a comprehensive and well-planned approach. Key considerations include selecting the right MRP-II software solution, establishing data integration and accuracy, aligning business processes with MRP-II functionalities, providing training and support to users, and fostering cross-functional collaboration to ensure seamless integration of MRP-II across the organization.

Manufacturing Resource Planning-II (MRP-II) represents an advanced approach to resource planning in the manufacturing industry. By extending beyond material management and incorporating various resource planning components, MRP-II enables organizations to achieve optimal resource utilization, streamline production processes, and enhance overall operational efficiency. Gaining a thorough understanding of the principles and implementation considerations of MRP-II becomes crucial for organizations aiming to maximize the benefits of ERP in effectively managing manufacturing resources.

Distribution Requirement Planning (DRP)

Distribution Requirement Planning (DRP) is a crucial aspect of ERP systems in the context of supply chain management. It focuses on efficiently managing the distribution of goods from the manufacturer or central warehouse to the end customers or retail locations. DRP involves forecasting the demand for products, determining the optimal inventory levels at distribution centers, and coordinating the movement of goods to meet customer demands effectively.

The primary objective of DRP is to ensure that the right products are available at the right time and in the right quantities at each distribution point. By accurately forecasting demand and aligning inventory levels with customer requirements, organizations can avoid stockouts and overstocking situations, resulting in improved customer satisfaction and cost savings.

DRP involves several key steps in the distribution planning process. Firstly, demand is forecasted based on historical sales data, market trends, and customer orders. This forecast serves as the foundation for determining the quantity and timing of product distribution. The next step is to calculate the replenishment needs at each distribution center by considering factors such as lead times, transportation constraints, and safety stock requirements.

Once the replenishment needs are determined, DRP systems generate replenishment orders to transfer or deliver products from the manufacturer or central warehouse to the distribution centers. These orders take into account the existing inventory levels, inbound shipments, and customer demand patterns. The DRP system continuously monitors inventory levels and adjusts replenishment orders to maintain optimal stock levels and meet customer demands efficiently.

Effective DRP implementation requires integration with other modules of the ERP system, such as inventory management, procurement, and sales. Integration enables real-time visibility into inventory levels, order processing, and customer demand across the supply chain, allowing organizations to make informed decisions and respond quickly to changes in demand or supply.

By leveraging DRP within an ERP system, organizations can streamline their distribution processes, minimize stockouts, reduce inventory holding costs, optimize transportation logistics, and enhance overall supply chain efficiency. This results in improved customer service, reduced lead times, and increased profitability for the organization.

DRP is a critical component of ERP systems that enables organizations to effectively manage the distribution of goods and meet customer demands. By accurately forecasting demand, optimizing inventory levels, and coordinating the movement of goods, organizations can achieve efficient distribution operations, enhance customer satisfaction, and drive business success.

Just-In-Time (JIT) and Kanban System

Just-In-Time (JIT) and the Kanban system are two powerful concepts in manufacturing that contribute to improved efficiency, reduced waste, and enhanced productivity. Both JIT and Kanban focus on optimizing inventory management and production processes to achieve a smooth flow of materials and minimize inventory holding costs.

Just-In-Time (JIT) is a philosophy that aims to produce and deliver products or components at the precise moment they are needed in the production process. It emphasizes eliminating waste, including excess inventory, overproduction, waiting times, and unnecessary transportation. By synchronizing production with customer demand, JIT enables organizations to minimize inventory levels, reduce lead times, and improve production efficiency. JIT relies on several key principles, such as continuous improvement, flexibility, standardization, and close collaboration with suppliers.

The Kanban system, on the other hand, is a visual signaling system that supports the implementation of JIT principles. Kanban, which means "visual card" or "signal" in Japanese, uses physical or digital cards or signals to trigger the replenishment of materials or components. Each production process or work center has a designated number of Kanban cards representing the quantity of items that can be held in that area. As products are consumed or moved to the next process, the Kanban cards are returned, signaling the need for replenishment. This creates a pull-based system, where production is driven by actual demand rather than predetermined schedules.

The Kanban system provides several benefits. It improves visibility and transparency throughout the production process, allowing teams to identify bottlenecks, balance workloads, and detect inefficiencies. Kanban promotes a culture of continuous improvement and collaboration by encouraging teams to regularly review and optimize their workflows. It enables organizations to manage inventory levels effectively, ensuring that materials are available when needed while minimizing excess stock. By reducing inventory and streamlining production, organizations can achieve shorter lead times, faster response to changes in customer demand, and improved overall productivity.

Implementing JIT and the Kanban system requires careful planning and coordination. It involves analyzing the production flow, identifying critical processes, establishing appropriate inventory levels, and setting up clear Kanban signals and rules.

Effective communication and collaboration between different departments and suppliers are essential to ensure the smooth operation of the system.

JIT and the Kanban system have been widely adopted across various industries, including manufacturing, logistics, and service sectors. They have proven to be effective strategies for reducing waste, improving quality, increasing efficiency, and enhancing customer satisfaction. Organizations that embrace JIT and the Kanban system can achieve significant cost savings, operational excellence, and a competitive edge in the market.

JIT and the Kanban system are integral components of lean manufacturing principles. They enable organizations to streamline production, reduce waste, and improve overall efficiency. By adopting a pull-based approach and visual signaling system, organizations can optimize inventory levels, minimize lead times, and respond quickly to customer demands. Implementing JIT and the Kanban system requires careful planning, strong collaboration, and continuous improvement efforts. However, the benefits in terms of cost savings, productivity gains, and customer satisfaction make them valuable strategies for organizations striving for operational excellence in the manufacturing realm.

Process Management

Process management is a crucial aspect of ERP, as it focuses on optimizing and improving the various business processes within an organization. It involves the identification, design, implementation, and continuous improvement of processes to enhance operational efficiency, reduce costs, and deliver value to customers.

Effective process management begins with process identification and documentation. This entails mapping out the current processes, understanding the inputs, outputs, activities, and dependencies involved, and documenting them in a standardized format. Process documentation serves as a foundation for process improvement efforts and provides a clear understanding of how different processes interconnect within the organization.

Once the processes are identified and documented, the next step is process analysis and redesign. This involves evaluating the current processes to identify bottlenecks, inefficiencies, and areas for improvement. By analyzing key performance indicators (KPIs), organizations can gain insights into process performance and identify opportunities for enhancement. Process redesign aims to eliminate non-value-added activities, simplify complex processes, and optimize resource utilization. It may involve resequencing tasks, introducing automation, or redefining roles and responsibilities to streamline the flow of work.

After process redesign, the implementation phase begins. This involves executing the redesigned processes and ensuring that employees understand their roles and responsibilities. It may require providing training and support to employees to adapt to the changes. During the implementation phase, organizations also need to establish monitoring and control mechanisms to track process performance and identify deviations from the desired outcomes. This enables timely intervention and corrective actions to maintain process efficiency and effectiveness.

Continuous improvement is a vital component of process management. Organizations should regularly review and evaluate their processes to identify further opportunities for optimization. This can be done through techniques such as process audits, customer feedback, employee suggestions, and benchmarking against industry best practices. By fostering a culture of continuous improvement, organizations can drive innovation, increase agility, and adapt to changing market dynamics.

ERP play a significant role in facilitating process management. They provide the technology infrastructure to support process automation, data integration, and real-time monitoring. ERP capture and store data from various departments and processes, enabling organizations to analyze process performance and make data-driven decisions. Additionally, ERP can enforce standardization and consistency across processes, ensuring that best practices are followed throughout the organization.

ERP provide the necessary tools and capabilities to support process automation, data integration, and real-time monitoring. By adopting effective process management practices, organizations can streamline operations, reduce costs, and improve overall performance.

Work Management

Work management is a critical aspect of ERP, focusing on effectively managing and coordinating the tasks, activities, and resources involved in day-to-day operations within an organization. It encompasses the planning, scheduling, execution, and monitoring of work processes to ensure smooth operations, optimal resource utilization, and timely completion of tasks.

One of the key components of work management in ERP is work planning. This involves identifying the tasks required to achieve specific objectives, setting priorities, and allocating resources accordingly. Work planning provides a roadmap for employees, outlining what needs to be done, when, and by whom. It helps in organizing workloads, avoiding bottlenecks, and ensuring that critical tasks are given due attention.

Work scheduling is another essential aspect of work management. It involves assigning tasks to individuals or teams and establishing timelines and deadlines for their completion. ERP provide functionalities to create and manage work schedules, taking into account resource availability, dependencies between tasks, and other constraints. Efficient work scheduling ensures that resources are utilized optimally, and tasks are completed within the desired timeframe.

Once work is planned and scheduled, the execution phase begins. Work management in ERP involves tracking the progress of tasks, monitoring milestones, and ensuring that work is being carried out as planned. ERP provide real-time visibility into the status of tasks, allowing managers to monitor progress, identify potential delays, and take corrective actions promptly. This enables proactive management and reduces the risk of project delays or disruptions.

Collaboration and communication are integral to effective work management. ERP provide centralized platforms for employees to collaborate, share information, and communicate with each other. This facilitates seamless coordination among team members, reduces information silos, and improves overall efficiency. Through ERP, employees can access relevant documents, updates, and discussions related to their work, enhancing collaboration and ensuring everyone is aligned with the project objectives.

Work management in ERP also involves performance tracking and measurement. ERP capture and store data related to work activities, allowing organizations to analyze performance metrics, such as task completion time, resource utilization, and quality of work. This data-driven approach enables organizations to identify areas for improvement, optimize work processes, and make informed decisions to enhance productivity and efficiency.

ERP provide features for work history management, enabling organizations to maintain records of completed tasks, project milestones, and related documentation. This historical data can be valuable for future reference, audits, performance evaluation, and continuous improvement initiatives.

By effectively managing work processes, organizations can optimize resource utilization, enhance productivity, and achieve desired outcomes efficiently.

Workflow Management

Workflow management plays a crucial role in optimizing business processes and streamlining operations within an organization. It involves the design, automation, execution, and monitoring of workflows to ensure that tasks and activities are efficiently carried out, resources are utilized effectively, and information flows seamlessly across departments and individuals. ERP provide robust workflow management capabilities that empower organizations to achieve greater operational efficiency and productivity.

One of the primary objectives of workflow management in ERP is to automate and standardize business processes. ERP enables the modeling and documentation of workflows, defining the sequence of tasks, the roles and responsibilities of individuals involved, and the flow of information and approvals. By automating these processes, organizations can reduce manual efforts, eliminate errors, and ensure consistency in the execution of tasks. ERP workflows can be customized to align with specific business requirements, enabling organizations to create efficient and tailored processes.

Another important aspect of workflow management in ERP is task assignment and tracking. ERP facilitate the assignment of tasks to individuals or teams based on predefined rules or conditions.

Tasks can be automatically routed to the appropriate personnel, ensuring that the right people are responsible for specific activities. ERP workflows provide real-time visibility into the status of tasks, allowing managers and stakeholders to monitor progress, identify bottlenecks, and take corrective actions as necessary. This transparency improves accountability, enhances collaboration, and enables timely decision-making.

ERP workflow management also supports exception handling and escalation. In complex business processes, exceptions or deviations from the standard workflow may occur. ERP allow organizations to define rules and conditions for handling these exceptions, ensuring that they are addressed promptly and efficiently. Escalation mechanisms can be set up to ensure that unresolved issues are brought to the attention of higher-level authorities for resolution. This helps organizations maintain control over their processes, minimize delays, and prevent potential disruptions.

Collaboration and communication are integral to effective workflow management in ERP. ERP provide centralized platforms for individuals and teams to collaborate, share information, and communicate throughout the workflow. Through integrated messaging systems, notifications, and document sharing capabilities, ERP facilitates smooth information exchange and decision-making within the workflow. This enables cross-functional collaboration, reduces information silos, and promotes efficient teamwork.

ERP workflow management supports performance monitoring and analysis. Workflow data captured within the ERP system allows organizations to analyze process performance metrics, such as task completion time, cycle time, and resource utilization. These insights help identify process bottlenecks, inefficiencies, and areas for improvement. By leveraging these analytics, organizations can optimize workflows, enhance productivity, and drive continuous process improvement initiatives.

By leveraging ERP's workflow management capabilities, organizations can standardize processes, automate routine tasks, improve collaboration, and monitor performance. This leads to increased operational efficiency, enhanced productivity, and the ability to adapt and respond to changing business needs effectively.

Work History Management

Work history management provides a comprehensive historical log of tasks, actions, and changes made within the ERP system, enabling organizations to review, analyze, and reference past work activities. This functionality is essential for various reasons, including compliance, auditability, problem-solving, and decision-making.

Within an ERP system, work history management captures and stores detailed information about transactions, processes, and system interactions. It records the date and time of each activity, the user or system account involved, and any relevant details or changes made. This historical data becomes a valuable resource for organizations, as it allows them to reconstruct past events, understand the sequence of activities, and investigate any issues or discrepancies that may have occurred.

One of the primary benefits of work history management in ERP is its contribution to compliance and audit requirements. Organizations often need to adhere to industry regulations, legal obligations, or internal policies that mandate the retention of historical data. With ERP, organizations can maintain a reliable audit trail of activities, demonstrating compliance with relevant standards and providing evidence of adherence to regulations. In the event of an audit or investigation, the work history can be used to validate processes, identify any non-compliance, and take corrective actions.

Work history management also supports problem-solving and issue resolution within ERP. When unexpected errors or discrepancies arise, having access to the complete work history allows organizations to trace the root cause, identify contributing factors, and troubleshoot effectively. By examining the sequence of activities leading up to an issue, organizations can determine the actions that may have caused the problem and take appropriate measures to prevent its recurrence. Work history provides a valuable reference point for analyzing and resolving system-related issues, improving overall system performance, and minimizing disruptions.

Work history management in ERP enhances decision-making capabilities. Historical data can be used to analyze trends, identify patterns, and gain insights into operational performance. By reviewing the work history, organizations can evaluate the effectiveness of certain processes, measure productivity, and identify areas for improvement. This information allows management to make data-driven decisions, implement process enhancements, and optimize resource allocation. Work history management empowers organizations to learn from past experiences, refine their strategies, and drive continuous improvement.

Work history management supports knowledge sharing and collaboration within an organization. As employees come and go, maintaining a comprehensive work history allows new team members to understand past activities, decisions, and outcomes. It facilitates knowledge transfer, promotes collaboration, and enables employees to build upon previous work. By accessing the work history, team members can gain insights, learn from past successes and failures, and leverage existing knowledge to achieve better outcomes. This promotes efficiency, avoids redundant efforts, and encourages a culture of continuous learning and innovation.

Work history management in ERP is an invaluable tool for organizations seeking to enhance their operational efficiency, drive continuous improvement, and leverage historical insights to achieve their business goals.

Product Data Management (PDM)

Product data management (PDM) enables organizations to effectively manage and control their product-related information throughout its lifecycle. PDM encompasses a range of processes and tools that facilitate the creation, storage, retrieval, and dissemination of accurate and up-to-date product data. It serves as a centralized repository for all product-related information, ensuring data integrity, consistency, and accessibility across the organization.

Within ERP, PDM provides a comprehensive solution for managing various aspects of product data, including BOMs, engineering change orders (ECOs), specifications, drawings, documentation, and other related information. It enables organizations to establish a structured and standardized approach to product data management, ensuring that accurate and consistent data is available to all stakeholders involved in the product lifecycle.

One of the key advantages of PDM in ERP is its ability to enhance collaboration and coordination among different departments and teams involved in product development and manufacturing. By centralizing product data within a unified system, PDM eliminates data silos and facilitates seamless information sharing across departments such as engineering, manufacturing, procurement, sales, and service. This promotes cross-functional collaboration, improves communication, and streamlines processes throughout the entire product lifecycle.

PDM also supports version control and revision management, ensuring that the most current and accurate product information is accessible to users. Through version control mechanisms, ERP enables organizations to maintain a complete history of changes made to product data, track revisions, and ensure that the latest approved versions are readily available. This helps prevent errors and inconsistencies caused by outdated or incorrect information, ultimately improving product quality and reducing the risk of costly rework or recalls.

Another key aspect of PDM in ERP is its ability to facilitate compliance with regulatory requirements and industry standards. For industries such as healthcare, automotive, aerospace, and consumer goods, adherence to specific regulations and standards is crucial. PDM allows organizations to manage product data in accordance with these requirements, ensuring that necessary certifications, documentation, and specifications are maintained and readily accessible. This not only helps organizations meet regulatory obligations but also enhances customer confidence and trust in the products they deliver.

PDM in ERP also enables organizations to streamline and automate various product-related processes, resulting in increased efficiency and productivity. For example, organizations can automate the generation of BOMs, streamline engineering change management, automate document control processes, and enable collaborative workflows. By automating these processes, organizations can reduce manual effort, minimize errors, and accelerate time-to-market for new products.

PDM in ERP provides valuable insights into product performance, usage, and customer feedback. By capturing and analyzing product data, organizations can gain a deeper understanding of customer preferences, market trends, and product performance metrics. This information can inform product development decisions, help identify opportunities for product improvement, and drive innovation.

PDM in ERP enables efficient product data management, fostering collaboration, compliance, and automation. It improves accuracy, streamlines processes, meets regulations, and drives innovation. PDM is vital for optimizing product management, delivering quality products, and gaining a competitive edge.

Table 1. Advantages and Disadvantages of Subtopics in ERP for Manufacturing

Sr. No.	Subtopic	Advantages	Disadvantages
1	Introduction to ERP in Manufacturing	Streamlines business processes, improves visibility and control, enhances data accuracy, facilitates decision-making.	Requires significant initial investment, complex implementation, potential resistance to change.
2	Material Requirement Planning (MRP)	Optimal inventory management, improved production planning, reduced stockouts, better resource utilization.	Requires accurate data inputs, dependence on forecast accuracy, can be resource-intensive to implement and maintain.
3	Manufacturing Resource Planning-II (MRP-II)	Comprehensive resource planning, effective capacity management, better production scheduling, enhanced cost control.	Complex implementation, requires accurate data inputs, potential resistance to change, ongoing maintenance and updates.

4	Distribution Requirement Planning (DRP)	Efficient inventory management, improved order fulfillment, optimized distribution network, reduced carrying costs.	Requires accurate demand forecasting, reliance on accurate data inputs, potential supply chain disruptions.
5	Just-In-Time (JIT) and Kanban System	Reduced inventory holding costs, improved production flow, enhanced quality control, minimized waste.	Requires synchronized supply chain, precise production planning, potential disruptions due to supply chain variability.
6	Process Management	Streamlined and standardized processes, improved efficiency, better quality control, reduced errors and rework.	Requires process analysis and reengineering, potential resistance to change, ongoing monitoring and optimization.
7	Work Management	Enhanced productivity, better resource allocation, improved task tracking and monitoring, streamlined workflows.	Initial setup and configuration, potential resistance to change, ongoing monitoring and maintenance.
8	Workflow Management	Streamlined approval processes, improved collaboration and coordination, reduced manual errors, enhanced visibility.	Requires process mapping and configuration, potential system complexity, ongoing maintenance and updates.
9	Work History Management	Better tracking and analysis of work history, improved performance evaluation, enhanced process improvement.	Requires comprehensive data capture, potential data privacy and security concerns, ongoing

				data management and analysis.
	10	Product Data Management (PDM)	Centralized product information, improved version control, enhanced collaboration, better data accuracy and accessibility.	Requires data standardization and maintenance, potential system integration challenges, ongoing data governance.

Tab.1 provides an overview of the advantages and disadvantages associated with ERP in manufacturing. It highlights the potential benefits and challenges organizations may encounter when implementing and utilizing these points in their manufacturing processes. It is important to note that the specific advantages and disadvantages can vary based on the organization's unique circumstances and requirements.

The topics discussed in this chapter are interconnected and represent different aspects of managing manufacturing operations through ERP systems. MRP helps organizations plan and manage their material needs, while MRP-II expands the scope to include resources and capacity planning. DRP focuses on managing the distribution of products efficiently. JIT and Kanban System aim to optimize inventory levels and production flow. Process Management, Work Management, Workflow Management, and Work History Management provide tools for managing and optimizing manufacturing processes. PDM ensures the effective management of product-related information throughout its lifecycle. Together, these topics highlight the comprehensive nature of ERP in addressing various aspects of manufacturing operations and enabling organizations to streamline processes, improve efficiency, and achieve their manufacturing goals.

Chapter 4 discusses the use of ERP and related technologies to improve business performance. These technologies include business process reengineering, data warehousing, data mining, supply chain management, and customer relationship management.

4

ERP and Related Technologies

In the previous chapter, we explored how ERP is applied in manufacturing businesses. Moving on to Chapter 4, our focus will be on "ERP and Related Technologies." This chapter will provide a detailed discussion on important topics like supply chain management, customer relationship management, data mining, and business process reengineering. Get ready to dive deeper into these subtopics as we broaden our understanding of ERP and its interconnected technologies.

Introduction

In the fast-evolving business environment of today, Organisations must use technology to improve their operations and stay competitive. The chapter will explore the fascinating field of "ERP and Related Technologies." We'll focus on crucial topics that are crucial for enhancing business operations and decision-making. We'll look at data mining, business process reengineering, data warehousing, supply chain management, customer relationship management, and data mining. We will learn crucial information about how ERP systems and related technology may alter businesses, boost productivity, and promote growth by looking at these interconnected areas. So join us on this instructive tour of the world of enterprise resource planning and its cutting-edge technical solutions.

Business Process Reengineering

The basic redesign and optimisation of business processes are the focus of business process reengineering (BPR), a crucial ERP concept, in order to produce noticeable gains in performance, efficiency, and customer satisfaction. BPR looks at current procedures, questions accepted theories, and imagines completely new business models. In order to eliminate inefficiencies, redundancies, and bottlenecks, businesses must undergo a paradigm shift in thinking that involves reevaluating every step of their process, from inputs and activities through outputs and outcomes.

The core objective of BPR is to abandon the constraints of antiquated procedures and adopt innovative methods that make use of ERP technology to organise business processes, reduce costs, and increase overall productivity. It requires reimagining how work is done and utilising the automation and integration characteristics of ERP systems to streamline procedures and foster interdepartmental communication.

Businesses must first determine the areas of their operations that need to be improved in order to start a successful BPR initiative. To do this, in-depth analyses of current workflows, new workflow charts, and the identification of pain points and inefficiencies are required. Understanding these challenges enables firms to design and create new, improved procedures that make the most of ERP's benefits.

To successfully implement BPR in an ERP environment, Effective change management, thorough preparation, and stakeholder participation are needed. Roles and responsibilities must be established, and organisational goals must be coordinated with ERP capabilities, and providing staff with proper training and assistance. To confirm the reengineered processes are producing the expected outcomes, ongoing monitoring, assessment, and change are also necessary.

BPR has many benefits when used within an ERP architecture. By optimising processes, eliminating pointless jobs, and adopting automation, businesses can improve operational efficiency, save costs, shorten cycle times, and increase customer satisfaction. BPR also gives businesses the flexibility they need to respond to shifting market conditions, take advantage of new opportunities, and maintain their competitiveness in challenging economic times.

It is critical to realise that BPR is a difficult endeavour that necessitates a thorough comprehension of the organization's particular needs, culture, and market dynamics. It necessitates flexibility, a dedication to constant improvement, and the ability to adapt to new commercial norms and technological advancements.

A revolutionary approach to improving company processes within the ERP framework is business process reengineering. By challenging conventional methods and utilising the power of ERP systems, organisations may significantly increase productivity, customer happiness, and efficiency. Stakeholder involvement, careful planning, and efficient change management are required for effective BPR implementation. BPR integration with ERP is worthwhile since it positions businesses for long-term success in a dynamic business environment.

When used to ERP, BPR requires carefully analysing and reanalysing processes to identify inefficiencies or bottlenecks. The following is included in this:

1. Process analysis and redesign: In order to find and address inefficiencies, business process reengineering (BPR) requires examining and redesigning present processes. The tools and features required to assess processes and look for room for improvement are provided by ERP systems.
2. Automation and integration: BPR aims to integrate data with ERP functionality while also automating manual processes. By automating tasks, businesses can improve productivity, decrease errors, and streamline procedures.
3. Change management and stakeholder engagement: Employees and stakeholders need to take a proactive role in the change process for BPR to succeed. ERP deployment usually requires significant organisational alterations, and Smooth transitions and high stakeholder engagement are ensured by effective change management involvement.
4. Perormance monitoring: In order to assess the effects of reengineered processes, BPR underlines the necessity of measuring and monitoring performance. ERP systems have dashboards and performance evaluation tools to monitor key metrics and evaluate the success of process improvements.
5. Organisational culture and mentality transformation: A change in organisational culture and mindset is necessary for BPR in order to embrace continual improvement and innovation. The deployment of ERP frequently alters how employees work, encouraging an active strategy for process evaluation and adaptation.

Data Warehousing

Data warehousing is the process of gathering data from several sources, combining it, and storing it in a central location for analysis and reporting. Data warehouses are widely used by ERP systems to store recent and old data from a range of sources, including financial systems, industrial systems, and CRM systems. To find patterns, follow trends, and make better business decisions, use this data.

The process of extracting data from multiple sources, translating it into a standardised format, and then loading it into a data warehouse is known as extraction, transformation, and loading (ETL).

The ETL process typically consists of the following steps:

1. Extraction: Data extraction from the source systems is the first stage in the ETL process. A number of techniques, such as file transfers, database queries, and web scraping, can be used to do this.
2. Transformation: The data must then be transformed into a consistent format. The data may need to be cleaned, duplicates removed, and converted to a standard data type.
3. Loading: The data warehouse must then be filled with the data. Numerous strategies, including mass loading and incremental loading, can be used to achieve this.

Data Warehousing in ERP Systems: Benefits

The advantages and difficulties of data warehousing in ERP systems are as follows:

1. Improved decision-making: By providing businesses with a single source of data truth, data warehousing can assist them in making better decisions. As a result, less time and effort will be required to collect and understand data from multiple sources.
2. Improved business intelligence: Businesses can learn about prior trends and patterns with the help of data warehousing. This information can be used to identify areas for development and guide future company decisions.
3. Improved customer service: By offering a deeper understanding of client preferences and wants, data warehousing can assist organisations in providing better customer service. This information can be used to improve the user experience and customer satisfaction.

Challenges of Data Warehousing in ERP Systems

1. Cost: Data warehouse implementation and upkeep can be expensive. The size and complexity of the business affect the cost of data warehousing.
2. Integration: In data warehousing, integrating data from several sources can be challenging. This is because different systems may use various data structures and formats.
3. Data quality: In data warehousing, it could be difficult to guarantee data quality. This is as a result of the potential for incomplete or faulty data.
4. Data mining and business intelligence: Building and running effective business intelligence and data mining applications in data warehousing can be challenging. This is because these applications demand particular knowledge and abilities.

Data warehousing can be a helpful tool for ERP systems despite the challenges. By properly creating and implementing a data warehouse, businesses may enhance their decision-making, business intelligence, and customer service.

Data warehousing has benefits for ERP systems. By properly creating and implementing a data warehouse, businesses may enhance their decision-making, business intelligence, and customer service.

Data Mining

Data mining is a potent ERP approach for drawing crucial conclusions and information from vast volumes of data. Employing potent algorithms and statistical models, data mining helps organisations to uncover hidden information and find patterns, trends, and linkages within their data. Data mining is essential in the context of ERP for enhancing decision-making, spotting fraud, and delivering better customer service.

One of the main advantages of data mining in ERP is better decision-making. By examining previous trends and patterns, businesses get important insights that aid in decision-making and the identification of potential areas for improvement in subsequent activities. Businesses can optimise their operations and produce growth thanks to this data.

The ability of ERP data mining to identify fraud is another advantage. By identifying suspicious trends and anomalies, such as several purchases made with the same credit card within a short period of time, data mining helps businesses avoid financial losses and safeguard themselves against fraudulent behaviour. This enhances the security and dependability of the ERP system.

Data mining enhances customer service. By studying their data, businesses can gain a deeper knowledge of the needs and preferences of their customers. They may customise their services, offer targeted marketing strategies, and produce wonderful customer experiences as a result of this insight. As a result, customer contentment increases, fostering long-term relationships and loyalty.

ERP systems face several challenges when it comes to data mining. One such issue is data quality. The accuracy and comprehensiveness of the underlying data influence how reliable the results of data mining are. Incomplete or inaccurate data might produce unreliable insights and obstruct wise decision-making. In order to ensure data integrity and quality throughout the data mining process, enterprises must do so.

Data mining is a difficult process that requires specialist knowledge and expertise. Knowledge of data mining strategies and tools is necessary for efficient data collecting, cleaning, and analysis. Organisations must train their workers or think about collaborating with professionals if they want to fully profit from data mining in ERP.

It can be expensive to develop and maintain data mining in ERP systems. The price varies depending on the complexity and size of the organisation. Budgets for the purchase of the necessary tools, the hiring of qualified individuals, and the maintenance of the infrastructure needed for data mining must be set aside by organisations. Prior to starting a data mining strategy, it is crucial to weigh the potential benefits against the associated expenses.

The practical applications of data mining in ERP can be illustrated with a number of instances. Data mining, for instance, can be used to forecast customer churn, enabling businesses to take preemptive measures to keep valuable customers. By identifying unusual activity patterns and halting fraudulent transactions, it can also aid in fraud detection. Customer segmentation, which enables businesses to classify consumers based on their preferences and modify marketing activities, is another application of data mining.

Additionally, demand forecasting using data mining can help businesses improve inventory management and better serve their customers.

Table 2   . Benefits and Challenges of Data Mining in ERP Systems

Benefits of Data Mining in ERP Systems	Challenges of Data Mining in ERP Systems
Improved decision-making	Data quality
Fraud detection	Complexity
Enhanced customer service	Cost
Identification of market trends	Privacy and security
Optimization of business processes	Interpretation of results

Tab. 2 highlights a review of the benefits and obstacles of integrating data mining in ERP systems.

In ERP systems, data mining is a crucial tool that helps with better decision-making, fraud detection, customer service, and a number of other tasks. Leveraging data mining's potential can help organisations acquire a competitive edge, identify opportunities, and accomplish their business objectives.

Supply Chain Management

ERP solutions must include supply chain management (SCM), which enables companies to optimise their supply chains and achieve operational excellence. SCM in ERP refers to the end-to-end management of the flow of information, resources, and items from the acquisition of raw materials to the delivery of the finished product to customers. It includes the coordination and integration of multiple operations, including order fulfilment, inventory management, production planning, and logistics.

Making sure that commodities move smoothly and efficiently across the supply chain is one of the main objectives of SCM in ERP. These include things like demand forecasting, inventory management, production scheduling, and logistics for transportation. By incorporating these operations into their ERP system, businesses may have real-time visibility into their supply chain, enabling them to make informed decisions, react quickly to shifting customer demands, and optimise inventory levels.

ERP systems give stakeholders a consolidated platform for controlling the whole supply chain, facilitating easy collaboration and communication. SCM in ERP can help businesses strengthen their relationships with suppliers, modernise the procurement process, and enhance supplier performance. By incorporating supplier data into the ERP system, businesses can keep track of deliveries, evaluate supplier performance, and guarantee that materials are restocked on schedule.

Businesses can increase customer satisfaction by improving order management and fulfilment processes with SCM in ERP. With real-time inventory information, businesses can accurately guarantee delivery dates to customers, cut down on order lead times, and manage order revisions more effectively. Better customer service and increased client loyalty are the benefits of this. Analyses of the supply chain are yet another crucial component of SCM in ERP. ERP systems equip businesses with powerful analytical tools that let them examine data from the supply chain, spot trends, and make decisions based on that data. By utilising these analytical skills, organisations may enhance supply chain performance, pinpoint problem areas, and promote continuing process changes.

ERP SCM installation is not without challenges. It can be challenging and time-consuming to integrate supply chain activities across several functional areas and departments; this calls for careful planning and coordination. In SCM, data consistency and quality are crucial since inaccurate or missing data can cause supply chain disruptions and inefficiencies. Furthermore, it is crucial to ensure data security and protect private supply chain information. SCM in ERP enables businesses to create flexible, adaptable supply chains that can successfully meet customer demands and experience long-term growth in an unstable economic environment.

Here are a few examples of how SCM might benefit from ERP systems:

1. Inventory management: ERP systems may help firms optimise their inventory levels by monitoring demand and supply. This can help businesses prevent stockouts and cut carrying costs.
2. Production planning: ERP systems can help businesses manage their production schedules in accordance with demand. This can help businesses cut costs and prevent overproduction.
3. Warehousing: ERP solutions can help businesses manage their warehouses more effectively by monitoring inventory levels and streamlining picking and packing. This can assist businesses in cutting costs while improving customer service.
4. Transportation: ERP systems, which track shipments and optimise routes, can help businesses manage their transportation more effectively. This can assist businesses in cutting costs while improving customer service.

By using ERP systems to optimise SCM, businesses can gain a competitive advantage and increase their bottom line.

Customer Relationship Management

ERP systems must include CRM (Customer Relationship Management) functionality. It encompasses techniques, procedures, and technological advancements that let companies manage and enhance their interactions with clients during the course of the client relationship. By integrating CRM capabilities within ERP systems, organisations may expedite their customer-related operations and gain crucial insights to increase customer satisfaction and drive corporate success.

One of the main goals of CRM in ERP is to centralise customer information and offer a complete picture of each customer's interactions and preferences. By merging customer data from several touchpoints, including sales, marketing, and customer support, ERP-based CRM enables a comprehensive picture of client behaviour and requests. Teamwork is made possible and consistent customer experiences are delivered thanks to this unified data store, which ensures that all departments have correct and recent client information.

ERP-based CRM systems enable more efficient lead and opportunity management. From lead creation to conversion, businesses may methodically track and manage potential sales prospects. By recording and assessing client contacts, CRM powered by ERP enables businesses to prioritise leads, effectively assign sales employees, and monitor the status of each opportunity. This increases the likelihood that sales teams will close deals by allowing them to focus their efforts on high-value prospects.

Businesses may develop individualised communication plans and targeted marketing campaigns thanks to CRM integration in ERP systems. Based on customer information like purchase history, preferences, and demographics, businesses can segment their customer base and customise marketing messages. Accurate targeting is made possible by CRM built on ERP, increasing the relevance and efficiency of marketing initiatives. The interaction with customers, reaction times, and conversion rates are all improved by this capability.

Businesses may develop targeted marketing campaigns and individualised communication strategies thanks to CRM integration in ERP systems. Based on customer information like purchase history, tastes, and demographics, organisations can segment their clientele and customise marketing messages. CRM powered by ERP offers precise targeting, increasing the relevance and efficiency of marketing initiatives. With this capability, customer interaction, response rates, and conversion rates are all improved.

Analysis of key performance indicators (KPIs) relating to customer relationships is also facilitated by CRM systems built on ERP. By assessing statistics like client lifetime value, churn rate, and customer acquisition cost, businesses can gain insights into the effectiveness of their CRM operations. To enhance customer interactions and overall business performance, these insights help identify areas for improvement, optimise resource allocation, and make data-driven decisions.

A CRM deployment within an ERP system presents additional challenges. Organisations must manage data consistency and quality across all departments to remove inconsistencies and errors in customer information. Precision configuration and synchronisation may be required for integration with third-party systems, such as marketing automation software or consumer feedback platforms. To ensure that staff members successfully use and benefit from the CRM capabilities, user adoption and training are crucial.

CRM in ERP systems is a potent tool that helps businesses effectively manage and grow their client connections. By integrating

CRM functionality, businesses may centralise customer data, enhance lead and opportunity management, tailor marketing campaigns, streamline customer care, and gain crucial insights for ongoing development. ERP-based CRM systems allow businesses to deliver exceptional customer experiences, encourage customer loyalty, and promote business success in the cutthroat environment of today.

In Chapter 4 of the book "ERP and Related Technologies," we covered a wide range of topics that illuminated how ERP systems affect companies.

We'll go more into the key elements of an ERP system in Chapter 5, highlighting their importance in facilitating effective data management, process automation, integration, and reporting inside an organisation.

5

Components of ERP systems

In Chapter 4 of the book "ERP and Related Technologies," we delved into several important topics that are relevant to ERP systems and their impact on organizations. Chapter 5 of the book "ERP and Related Technologies" focuses on the essential components that constitute ERP systems. This chapter delves into the core elements that enable ERP systems to streamline operations, enhance collaboration, and facilitate data-driven decision-making. We will explore the concept of an enterprise-wide database, the significance of business process automation, the integration of functional areas, and the role of reporting and analytics. By gaining insights into these components, readers will gain a deeper understanding of how ERP systems function and the value they bring to organizations.

Introduction

In this chapter, we will explore the key components that form the foundation of ERP systems. These components include the enterprise-wide database, business process automation, integration of functional areas, and reporting and analytics. By understanding these crucial elements, you will gain insights into how ERP systems enable organizations to centralize and integrate their data, automate critical processes, facilitate cross-functional collaboration, and leverage data-driven insights for informed decision-making. Join us on this journey as we delve into the essential components of ERP systems and uncover their transformative potential in driving organizational efficiency and effectiveness.

Enterprise-wide database

An enterprise-wide database refers to a centralized repository that stores and manages all the organizational data related to various functional areas and processes within an organization. It serves as a comprehensive and integrated database that collects, organizes, and maintains structured and unstructured data from different departments, such as finance, human resources, sales, marketing, and operations.

The enterprise-wide database plays a crucial role in ERP systems by providing a unified view of data across the entire organization. It eliminates data redundancy and duplication by consolidating data from different systems and applications into a single database. This consolidation enhances data integrity, consistency, and accuracy throughout the ERP system.

By having a centralized database, the enterprise-wide database enables seamless information sharing and collaboration among different departments. It supports cross-functional visibility and analysis, allowing stakeholders to access and analyze data from various functional areas, facilitating informed decision-making and fostering better collaboration among teams.

The enterprise-wide database supports real-time data updates and synchronization, ensuring that users have access to up-to-date and accurate information. This real-time data availability enhances the agility and responsiveness of the organization, enabling timely responses to market changes, customer demands, and internal operational needs.

The enterprise-wide database also plays a significant role in data security and access controls. It ensures that data is appropriately protected through defined user roles and permissions, safeguarding sensitive information and ensuring compliance with data privacy regulations.

Here are some of the key features and benefits of an enterprise-wide database:

1. Central repository of organizational data: The enterprise-wide database consolidates data from various functional areas and departments, eliminating redundancy and duplication. By providing a unified view of data, it ensures consistency and accuracy throughout the ERP system. This central repository acts as a single source of truth, supporting reliable decision-making and reducing complexity in data management.
2. Cross-functional visibility and analysis: Integration of data from multiple functional areas enables cross-functional visibility and analysis. The enterprise-wide database facilitates the alignment of business processes across departments, allowing for a holistic view of organizational operations. This cross-functional perspective enhances decision-making by providing insights into the interconnectedness of different business functions.
3. Real-time data updates and synchronization: The enterprise-wide database supports real-time data updates and synchronization, enabling timely and accurate information sharing. This real-time data availability enhances organizational agility and responsiveness, allowing for faster responses to market changes and internal needs. Real-time data also facilitates collaboration and coordination among

departments, ensuring everyone has access to the latest information.

4. Data security and access controls: The enterprise-wide database ensures data security through user roles and permissions. It protects sensitive information and ensures compliance with data privacy regulations. By defining access controls, organizations can safeguard their data and prevent unauthorized access or manipulation.

5. Advanced analytics and reporting: The enterprise-wide database serves as a rich data source for advanced analytics and reporting capabilities. It enables the generation of meaningful insights, identification of trends and patterns, and data-driven decision-making. By leveraging the data stored in the enterprise-wide database, organizations can gain valuable insights into their operations, performance, and customer behavior.

6. Integration with other ERP modules: The enterprise-wide database seamlessly integrates with other ERP modules, enabling the flow of data between different functional areas. This integration enhances process automation, efficiency, and overall system performance. It ensures that data from various modules is synchronized and accessible to support end-to-end business processes.

Here are some of the considerations for implementing and managing an enterprise-wide database:

1. Data governance and data quality: Implementing effective data governance practices is essential for the enterprise-wide database. Organizations should establish data management policies, standards, and processes to ensure data integrity and quality. This includes data cleansing, enrichment, and ongoing maintenance procedures.

2. Scalability and performance optimization: As data volumes increase, the enterprise-wide database must be scalable and optimized for performance. This involves designing a robust database architecture, implementing optimization techniques, and regularly monitoring and tuning performance to ensure efficient data processing and retrieval.
3. Integration with external systems and data sources: The enterprise-wide database should support integration with external systems and data sources. This includes integrating with third-party applications and data providers to enable data synchronization and exchange. Seamless integration with external systems enhances data completeness and accuracy within the ERP system.

By considering these factors, organizations can implement and manage an enterprise-wide database that meets their specific needs and drives business success.

Business process automation

Business process automation in the context of ERP refers to the use of technology to streamline and automate various business processes within an organization. ERP systems provide a centralized platform that integrates different functional areas and modules, enabling organizations to automate and optimize their operations.

One of the primary objectives of business process automation within ERP is to eliminate manual and repetitive tasks. By leveraging software tools and systems, organizations can replace manual data entry, calculations, and document generation with automated workflows. This automation not only reduces human error but also saves time and improves overall operational efficiency.

ERP systems enable the design and implementation of workflows that define the sequence of tasks and activities involved in a specific business process. These workflows automate the routing of information and documents, ensuring that tasks are completed in a predefined order and that relevant stakeholders are notified at each step. By automating workflows, organizations can standardize processes and ensure consistent execution, leading to increased productivity and reduced cycle times.

Integration and data exchange are crucial aspects of business process automation within ERP. ERP systems integrate various functional areas, such as finance, supply chain, human resources, and manufacturing, into a single system. This integration allows for seamless data exchange between processes, eliminating the need for manual data entry and ensuring data consistency across the organization. For example, when a customer order is received, the ERP system can automatically update inventory levels, initiate the procurement process, and generate invoices, eliminating the need for manual intervention and improving process efficiency.

Automated alerts and notifications play a vital role in business process automation within ERP. ERP systems can generate alerts and notifications to inform relevant stakeholders about critical events or when certain conditions are met. For instance, if an inventory item reaches a predefined threshold, the system can automatically trigger a notification to the procurement department to initiate a reorder. These alerts and notifications enable proactive decision-making and ensure timely action, improving overall responsiveness and customer satisfaction.

Monitoring and reporting capabilities are essential for effective business process automation within ERP. ERP systems provide real-time dashboards and reports that allow managers to monitor the performance of automated processes. By analyzing key performance indicators, managers can gain insights into process efficiency, identify bottlenecks, and make data-driven decisions for process optimization and continuous improvement. This monitoring and reporting capability enables organizations to drive operational excellence and adapt to changing business needs.

Business process automation within ERP offers numerous benefits to organizations. It increases productivity by freeing employees from manual and repetitive tasks, allowing them to focus on higher-value activities. It reduces errors and improves data accuracy by eliminating manual data entry. It enhances process visibility and transparency, enabling organizations to track and measure performance. It ensures compliance with regulatory requirements by enforcing standardized processes. Additionally, it leads to cost savings through improved resource allocation and operational efficiency.

Table 3. Advantages and Disadvantages of Business Process Automation in ERP

Advantages	Disadvantages
1. Increased efficiency and productivity	1. Initial implementation cost and complexity
2. Reduced errors and improved accuracy	2. Potential resistance to change
3. Faster process execution and cycle times	3. Dependence on technology and system uptime
4. Standardized and consistent processes	4. Potential job displacement and retraining
5. Enhanced scalability and capacity	5. Limited flexibility for ad-hoc scenarios
6. Improved data visibility and reporting	6. Potential security and privacy concerns
7. Streamlined compliance and regulatory adherence	7. Risk of process rigidity and lack of agility
8. Better resource allocation and utilization	8. Continuous maintenance and updates

Tab. 3 presents the key advantages and disadvantages of implementing business process automation in the context of ERP systems. It highlights the benefits organizations can achieve through automation as well as potential challenges to consider during implementation and operation.

Business process automation within ERP is a strategic approach that leverages technology to streamline and automate business processes. It eliminates manual tasks, standardizes workflows, integrates functional areas, and provides real-time visibility and analytics. By embracing business process automation within their ERP systems, organizations can achieve greater efficiency, productivity, and competitiveness in today's dynamic business environment.

Integration of functional areas

Integration of functional areas is a crucial aspect of ERP systems that aims to streamline and optimize organizational processes by connecting different departments and functions. It involves the synchronization and harmonization of data, workflows, and activities across various functional areas within an organization.

One of the primary objectives of integrating functional areas in ERP is to eliminate data silos and ensure the availability of consistent and up-to-date information. By integrating data from departments such as finance, human resources, sales, marketing, and operations, organizations can achieve a comprehensive view of their operations. This integration allows for better coordination, collaboration, and decision-making across functions, leading to improved efficiency and effectiveness in overall business operations.

In addition to data integration, the integration of functional areas also involves aligning and automating business processes. ERP systems provide a platform for mapping, standardizing, and automating processes that span different departments. By automating routine tasks and workflows, organizations can reduce manual effort, minimize errors, and improve process efficiency. For example, a sales order generated in the sales department can automatically trigger activities in other departments such as inventory management, production planning, and accounting, ensuring a seamless flow of information and actions.

Integration of functional areas enables organizations to achieve better control and visibility over their operations. ERP systems provide real-time insights into the status of various activities, enabling managers to monitor performance, track key metrics, and make informed decisions. The integration of functional areas allows for a holistic view of the organization, facilitating cross-functional reporting and analysis. Decision-makers can access integrated reports and analytics that provide a comprehensive understanding of the interdependencies and impacts of different functions on overall performance.

Achieving successful integration of functional areas within an ERP system can present challenges. These challenges include managing data mappings and conversions, ensuring data consistency and accuracy across functions, addressing resistance to change from employees, and handling complex customization and configuration requirements. Organizations must invest in proper planning, training, and change management strategies to mitigate these challenges and maximize the benefits of functional integration.

Integration of functional areas in ERP systems is essential for organizations to achieve a unified and streamlined approach to their operations. It involves connecting data, processes, and activities across departments to eliminate silos, enhance collaboration, automate workflows, and improve decision-making. By implementing effective integration strategies, organizations can optimize their resources, improve efficiency, and gain a competitive advantage in the market.

The process of integrating functional areas within an ERP system involves several steps to ensure a seamless flow of information and processes across different departments. The following is a detailed outline of the typical steps involved in the integration process:

1. Define Integration Objectives: Clearly identify the goals and objectives of the integration project. Determine the specific functional areas that need to be integrated and the desired outcomes of the integration.
2. Conduct a Business Process Analysis: Analyze and document the existing business processes within each functional area. Identify areas of overlap, dependencies, and potential bottlenecks. This analysis will serve as the foundation for designing the integrated processes.
3. Map Data and Process Flows: Create a visual representation of the data and process flows between different functional areas. Identify the inputs, outputs, and dependencies of each process. This mapping exercise helps in identifying gaps and areas that require integration.
4. Standardize Data and Processes: Establish standardized data formats, naming conventions, and process guidelines across functional areas. This step ensures consistency and compatibility in data exchange and process execution.
5. Design Integration Architecture: Determine the technical architecture and infrastructure required for integrating functional areas. Consider factors such as data integration methods (e.g., APIs, data connectors, middleware), system interoperability, and data synchronization mechanisms.

6. Develop Integration Interfaces: Build the necessary interfaces and connectors to facilitate data exchange and process integration between different systems or modules. This may involve developing custom integration modules, configuring middleware platforms, or leveraging pre-built connectors provided by the ERP system.
7. Test and Validate Integration: Conduct thorough testing to ensure the accuracy and reliability of the integrated processes. Verify that data flows correctly between different functional areas and that all dependencies and triggers are properly synchronized.
8. Implement and Deploy: Roll out the integrated system across the organization. Ensure proper training and change management strategies are in place to support the transition to the integrated processes.
9. Monitor and Fine-tune: Continuously monitor the integrated processes and address any issues or inefficiencies that arise. Fine-tune the integration settings, data mappings, and process flows based on feedback and real-world usage.
10. Continuous Improvement: Regularly review and optimize the integrated processes based on performance metrics, user feedback, and evolving business requirements. Look for opportunities to further streamline and enhance the integration to maximize the benefits.

Reporting and analytics

Reporting and analytics are essential components of ERP systems, enabling organizations to extract valuable insights from their data and make informed decisions. These capabilities have a significant impact on various aspects of an organization's operations. Firstly, reporting and analytics support data-driven decision-making by providing access to real-time and historical data. This enables decision-makers to analyze trends, patterns, and key performance indicators (KPIs), leading to a comprehensive understanding of business operations and the identification of areas for improvement and growth opportunities.

Reporting and analytics facilitate performance monitoring across different functional areas. Organizations can track their progress, measure key metrics, and compare performance against predefined benchmarks or targets. This visibility allows management to identify bottlenecks, inefficiencies, and areas of improvement, resulting in enhanced operational effectiveness.

Another important aspect is proactive problem identification. Reporting and analytics help organizations identify and address issues before they escalate. By monitoring critical metrics and analyzing data, potential problems can be detected in advance, enabling timely intervention and corrective actions. This proactive approach minimizes disruptions, optimizes processes, and improves overall business performance.

Strategic planning and forecasting are also empowered by reporting and analytics. By analyzing historical data, market trends, and customer behavior, organizations can develop data-driven strategies and make accurate forecasts. This enables them to anticipate future demands, optimize resource allocation, and align their strategies accordingly. The ability to plan strategically based on reliable data is essential for staying ahead of the competition and capitalizing on new business opportunities.

Reporting and analytics also play a role in compliance and governance. By generating accurate and comprehensive reports, organizations can demonstrate compliance with regulatory requirements and track audit trails. This ensures transparency in operations, particularly in industries with stringent regulatory frameworks. Compliance and governance are critical for maintaining trust, managing risk, and protecting the organization's reputation.

Reporting and analytics support a culture of continuous improvement. By analyzing data on key performance indicators, organizations can identify areas for process optimization, cost reduction, and productivity improvement. This continuous improvement mindset helps streamline operations, enhance customer satisfaction, and achieve sustainable growth.

Reporting and analytics are vital in ERP systems as they enable data-driven decision-making, performance monitoring, proactive problem identification, strategic planning and forecasting, compliance and governance, and continuous improvement. These capabilities empower organizations to leverage their data effectively, optimize operations, and drive business success.

In the context of ERP systems, reporting and analytics are essential components that provide valuable insights into organizational data. These capabilities enable businesses to extract meaningful information, identify trends, and make informed decisions. There are various types of reports and analytics available within an ERP system, each serving a specific purpose and providing unique insights. Let's explore some of the common types of reports and analytics in ERP:

Types of Reports and Analytics in ERP

1. Operational Reports: Operational reports focus on day-to-day activities and provide real-time information on key operational metrics. These reports include transactional data such as sales reports, purchase orders, inventory levels, and production status. Operational reports help monitor current

operations, identify bottlenecks, and facilitate timely operational decisions.
2. Financial Reports: Financial reports concentrate on the financial aspects of an organization. They include balance sheets, income statements, cash flow statements, and financial ratios. Financial reports offer insights into an organization's financial health, profitability, liquidity, and overall financial performance. They are crucial for financial planning, budgeting, and analysis.
3. Management Reports: Management reports are designed to support strategic decision-making by providing summarized and aggregated data on various aspects of the organization. These reports cover areas such as sales performance, customer satisfaction, employee productivity, and market trends. Management reports often include key performance indicators (KPIs) and visual representations of data to facilitate decision-making at the managerial level.
4. Ad-Hoc Reports: Ad-hoc reports are customized reports created on-demand to address specific information needs or answer specific business questions. These reports are flexible and tailored to the unique requirements of users. Ad-hoc reporting allows users to explore data, drill down into details, and analyze information from different perspectives.
5. Dashboards and Scorecards: Dashboards and scorecards provide a visual representation of key metrics and performance indicators. These tools offer a consolidated view of critical information in a graphical format, allowing users to quickly assess performance, identify trends, and make data-driven decisions. Dashboards often include charts, graphs, and gauges to present information in a visually appealing and easy-to-understand manner.

6. Predictive Analytics: Predictive analytics utilizes historical data and statistical algorithms to forecast future outcomes and trends. This type of analysis helps organizations anticipate demand, optimize resource allocation, and make proactive decisions. Predictive analytics can be used in areas such as sales forecasting, inventory management, and customer behavior analysis.
7. Data Mining and Business Intelligence: Data mining and business intelligence tools enable organizations to extract valuable insights from large datasets. These tools utilize advanced algorithms to discover patterns, correlations, and anomalies within the data. Data mining and business intelligence techniques are commonly used for market analysis, customer segmentation, and product recommendation.

These various types of reports and analytics within an ERP system provide organizations with valuable information to support decision-making, improve operational efficiency, and drive business growth. By leveraging the power of reporting and analytics, organizations can gain a competitive edge and make informed decisions based on reliable data.

Key Performance Indicators (KPIs) and Metrics

Key Performance Indicators (KPIs) and metrics are essential tools for measuring and evaluating the performance and progress of an organization. They provide quantifiable measurements that reflect the achievement of strategic goals and objectives. KPIs and metrics are used to monitor performance, identify areas for improvement, and make informed decisions. Here is a short summary note on KPIs and metrics:

KPIs represent the critical factors that are vital to the success of an organization. They are specific, measurable, and directly aligned with strategic objectives. KPIs are often used to track performance in key areas such as sales, customer satisfaction, operational efficiency, and financial performance. They provide a clear indication of whether an organization is on track to achieve its desired outcomes.

Metrics, on the other hand, are quantifiable measures used to assess performance and progress. They provide objective data and enable organizations to track their performance over time. Metrics can be financial, operational, customer-related, or employee-related. They provide a more detailed view of performance within specific areas and can be used to identify trends, patterns, and areas for improvement.

The selection of KPIs and metrics should be aligned with the organization's strategic objectives and should be meaningful and relevant to the specific industry and context. They should be specific, measurable, attainable, relevant, and time-bound (SMART). KPIs and metrics should also be regularly reviewed and updated to ensure they remain aligned with changing business priorities.

The use of KPIs and metrics enables organizations to monitor progress, set benchmarks, and make data-driven decisions. They provide a basis for performance evaluation, help identify areas of improvement, and enable organizations to focus on what matters most to achieve their strategic goals. KPIs and metrics play a crucial role in driving performance, fostering accountability, and supporting continuous improvement within organizations.

Data Visualization and Dashboards

Data visualization and dashboards are powerful tools that transform complex data into visual representations, making it easier to understand and interpret information. They provide a visual snapshot of key metrics, trends, and patterns, enabling organizations to gain insights and make informed decisions. Here is a short summary note on data visualization and dashboards:

Data visualization involves presenting data in graphical or visual formats such as charts, graphs, maps, and infographics. It goes beyond traditional tabular data and allows users to quickly grasp information, identify trends, and spot anomalies. Data visualization enhances data comprehension, promotes data exploration, and facilitates effective communication of insights across all levels of an organization.

Dashboards, on the other hand, are user interfaces that display key metrics and data visualizations in a consolidated and interactive manner. Dashboards provide a real-time overview of performance, enabling users to monitor progress, track KPIs, and identify areas of concern. They allow users to customize the view, drill down into specific data points, and interact with the data to gain deeper insights.

The benefits of data visualization and dashboards

1. Gain insights at a glance: Visual representations make it easier to identify patterns, correlations, and outliers in data, allowing for quick and intuitive decision-making.
2. Communicate information effectively: Visuals are often more impactful and memorable than raw data. They facilitate clear and concise communication of complex information to diverse audiences.

3. Foster data-driven decision-making: Data visualization and dashboards provide stakeholders with actionable insights, empowering them to make informed decisions based on real-time data.
4. Identify trends and anomalies: By visualizing data over time, organizations can identify trends, spot anomalies, and proactively address potential issues or opportunities.
5. Enhance collaboration and engagement: Data visualization and dashboards promote collaborative discussions around data, enabling teams to align their efforts and drive meaningful outcomes.

To fully leverage the benefits of data visualization and dashboards, organizations should ensure that visualizations are meaningful, accurate, and aligned with the intended audience. They should choose appropriate visualization techniques based on the type of data and the insights they want to convey. Regular review and refinement of dashboards are essential to ensure they remain relevant and useful in an ever-evolving business landscape.

Ad-Hoc Reporting and Customization

Ad-hoc reporting and customization are critical capabilities within ERP systems that empower users to create custom reports and analyze data according to their specific needs and requirements. Unlike predefined reports, ad-hoc reporting allows users to access and manipulate data in a flexible and self-service manner, enabling them to explore and derive insights from the data in real-time.

With ad-hoc reporting, users have the freedom to choose data sources, apply filters and criteria, and define report layouts and formats. They can drill down into detailed data, apply calculations and formulas, and visualize information using charts, graphs, and other graphical representations. This level of customization empowers users to answer unique business questions, identify trends, and make informed decisions based on their specific analytical goals.

Ad-hoc reporting offers several benefits to organizations. First and foremost, it promotes agility and responsiveness by reducing dependence on IT or technical teams to create custom reports. Users can directly access and analyze data, accelerating the decision-making process and enabling faster responses to changing business needs.

Ad-hoc reporting enhances user productivity and efficiency. It eliminates the need to sift through large volumes of data to find relevant information, as users can easily filter and sort data to focus on specific parameters. This capability saves time and effort, enabling users to focus on analyzing the data rather than preparing it.

Ad-hoc reporting encourages data exploration and discovery. Users can interactively manipulate and visualize data, uncovering hidden patterns, correlations, and outliers. This empowers them to gain deeper insights, identify opportunities, and address business challenges proactively.

While ad-hoc reporting provides significant flexibility and autonomy, organizations need to consider certain factors to ensure its effective implementation. Data governance is crucial to maintain data accuracy, consistency, and integrity across different reports and analyses. Establishing data governance processes, such as defining data standards and ensuring data quality, is essential to ensure reliable and trustworthy insights.

Organizations should provide adequate training and support to users to maximize the benefits of ad-hoc reporting. Users need to understand the capabilities of the reporting tools and be familiar with data structures and relationships within the ERP system. Offering training programs, documentation, and ongoing support will help users navigate and leverage ad-hoc reporting effectively.

Ad-hoc reporting and customization empower users within ERP systems to create tailored reports and analyze data according to their specific needs. It promotes agility, productivity, and data exploration, enabling users to make informed decisions and uncover valuable insights.

Integration of Reporting and Analytics with Other ERP Modules

Integration of reporting and analytics with other ERP modules is a crucial aspect of leveraging the full potential of an ERP system. By integrating reporting and analytics functionalities with various modules, such as finance, supply chain, human resources, and customer relationship management, organizations can gain comprehensive insights into their business operations and make informed decisions.

The integration enables seamless data flow between different modules, ensuring that relevant and up-to-date information is available for reporting and analysis purposes. This eliminates the need for manual data extraction and reconciliation, saving time and reducing the risk of errors.

By integrating reporting and analytics with other ERP modules, organizations can generate holistic reports that encompass multiple functional areas. For example, financial reports can incorporate data from sales, inventory, and procurement modules to provide a comprehensive view of the organization's financial health. This integration allows decision-makers to understand the impact of different business processes on financial outcomes and identify opportunities for improvement.

Integrating reporting and analytics with other ERP modules enables drill-down capabilities, where users can access detailed transactional data from various modules. This level of granularity facilitates root cause analysis, enabling users to identify the underlying factors contributing to specific outcomes or issues.

Integration also enhances data consistency and accuracy. Since data is sourced directly from the ERP system's modules, there is a single version of truth, reducing the chances of data discrepancies or inconsistencies across reports and analyses.

Integration enables real-time reporting and analysis. As data is continuously updated within the ERP system, reports and analytics can reflect the most recent information. This real-time access to data empowers decision-makers to make timely and informed decisions based on the current state of the business.

Integrating reporting and analytics with other ERP modules requires careful planning and consideration. Organizations need to ensure that data definitions and structures are standardized across modules to enable seamless integration. Data governance practices, such as data cleansing, data quality management, and metadata management, become crucial to maintain consistency and integrity.

Benefits of Reporting and Analytics in ERP

Reporting and analytics are essential components of ERP systems that offer numerous benefits to organizations. Here are some key benefits of reporting and analytics in ERP:

1. Informed Decision-Making: Reporting and analytics provide valuable insights and data visualizations that support informed decision-making. By analyzing data from various sources, organizations can identify trends, patterns, and correlations that help them make strategic and

operational decisions based on accurate and up-to-date information.

2. Real-Time Visibility: Reporting and analytics in ERP systems enable real-time data access, allowing organizations to monitor their performance and operations in real-time. This timely visibility into key metrics and KPIs empowers decision-makers to respond quickly to changing market conditions, identify bottlenecks, and take proactive measures to drive improvements.

3. Performance Monitoring: Reporting and analytics help organizations monitor their performance across different business functions, such as finance, sales, supply chain, and human resources. By tracking and analyzing performance indicators, organizations can identify areas of improvement, measure progress towards goals, and optimize processes to enhance overall performance and efficiency.

4. Data-Driven Insights: Reporting and analytics enable data-driven insights by providing a comprehensive view of organizational data. By combining data from multiple sources and performing advanced analytics techniques, organizations can uncover hidden patterns, correlations, and opportunities that drive innovation, process optimization, and competitive advantage.

5. Enhanced Transparency: Reporting and analytics promote transparency within an organization by providing accurate and accessible data to stakeholders. By sharing standardized reports and dashboards, organizations can improve communication, align objectives, and foster a data-driven culture where decisions are based on facts rather than assumptions.

6. Compliance and Risk Management: Reporting and analytics support compliance with regulatory requirements and

facilitate risk management. By generating reports that demonstrate adherence to industry regulations, organizations can ensure compliance and minimize the risk of penalties or legal issues. Analytics capabilities also help identify potential risks and vulnerabilities, enabling proactive risk mitigation strategies.

7. Continuous Improvement: Reporting and analytics foster a culture of continuous improvement by identifying areas for optimization and efficiency gains. Through data analysis, organizations can identify process bottlenecks, cost-saving opportunities, and areas of underperformance, enabling them to implement targeted improvement initiatives and drive operational excellence.

8. Customer Insights: Reporting and analytics enable organizations to gain deep insights into customer behavior, preferences, and satisfaction levels. By analyzing customer data, organizations can personalize their offerings, enhance customer experiences, and develop targeted marketing campaigns that drive customer retention and loyalty.

The benefits of reporting and analytics in ERP systems are numerous, ranging from informed decision-making and real-time visibility to performance monitoring, compliance management, and continuous improvement. By harnessing the power of data and analytics, organizations can drive operational efficiency, strategic growth, and competitive advantage in today's data-driven business landscape.

Challenges and Considerations in Reporting and Analytics Implementation

Challenges and Considerations in Reporting and Analytics Implementation require careful attention to data quality, security, resource requirements, change management, scalability, data governance, compliance, and alignment with user requirements to ensure successful implementation and maximize the value derived from reporting and analytics solutions.

Here are some challenges and considerations in reporting and analytics implementation:

1. Data Quality and Integration: One of the major challenges in reporting and analytics implementation is ensuring the quality and integration of data from various sources. Data inconsistencies, incomplete data, and data integration issues can hinder the accuracy and reliability of reports and analytics. Organizations need to invest in data cleansing, data governance, and data integration processes to address these challenges.
2. Data Security and Privacy: Reporting and analytics involve handling sensitive data, including financial information, customer data, and employee information. Ensuring data security and privacy is crucial to protect against unauthorized access, data breaches, and compliance violations. Organizations must implement robust security measures, access controls, and adhere to data privacy regulations when implementing reporting and analytics solutions.
3. Resource and Skill Requirements: Effective reporting and analytics implementation requires skilled resources, including data analysts, data scientists, and technical experts. Organizations may face challenges in recruiting and retaining these professionals, as they are in high demand. Adequate training and development programs should be in place to enhance the skills of existing resources and attract new talent.

4. Change Management: Implementing reporting and analytics systems often involves changes in processes, workflows, and user roles. Resistance to change and lack of user adoption can pose challenges to successful implementation. Organizations need to invest in change management strategies, including effective communication, training, and stakeholder engagement, to ensure smooth adoption of reporting and analytics solutions.
5. Scalability and Performance: As data volumes and complexity increase, scalability and performance become crucial considerations. Reporting and analytics systems should be able to handle large datasets, complex queries, and deliver results in a timely manner. Organizations should plan for scalability, invest in appropriate hardware and infrastructure, and regularly monitor and optimize performance to ensure smooth operations.
6. Data Governance and Compliance: Reporting and analytics implementation requires organizations to establish robust data governance practices to ensure data integrity, consistency, and compliance. This includes defining data ownership, data stewardship roles, and establishing data governance frameworks. Compliance with industry regulations and data privacy laws should also be a top consideration during implementation.
7. Business Alignment and User Requirements: It is essential to align reporting and analytics initiatives with business objectives and user requirements. Understanding the specific needs of different stakeholders, departments, and user roles is crucial to design and implement reports and analytics that provide actionable insights. Collaboration between IT and business teams is key to ensure that

reporting and analytics solutions meet user expectations and drive business value.

Best Practices for Effective Reporting and Analytics in ERP

To ensure effective reporting and analytics in ERP systems, organizations should follow best practices that focus on data governance, user-friendly visualization, scalability, training, and continuous improvement. By implementing these practices, organizations can harness the power of data to make informed decisions, drive performance improvements, and stay ahead in a competitive business landscape.

To ensure effective reporting and analytics in ERP systems, organizations can follow these best practices:

1. Define Clear Objectives: Clearly define the objectives and goals of reporting and analytics initiatives. Identify the key metrics and performance indicators that align with the organization's strategic priorities and objectives.
2. Establish Data Governance: Implement strong data governance practices to ensure data accuracy, integrity, and consistency. Define data ownership, establish data quality standards, and implement processes for data cleansing, validation, and maintenance.
3. Data Integration and Data Quality: Integrate data from various sources into a centralized data repository within the ERP system. Ensure data quality by performing data cleansing, normalization, and enrichment. Regularly monitor data quality to maintain the accuracy and reliability of reports and analytics.
4. User-Friendly Dashboards and Visualization: Design intuitive and user-friendly dashboards and data

visualizations that present information in a clear and concise manner. Use charts, graphs, and interactive visualizations to enable easy interpretation of data and insights.

5. Scalability and Performance: Ensure that the reporting and analytics infrastructure is scalable to handle increasing data volumes and user demands. Optimize performance by implementing indexing, caching, and query optimization techniques to ensure efficient data retrieval and processing.

6. Training and User Adoption: Provide comprehensive training and support to users on how to effectively use the reporting and analytics capabilities of the ERP system. Promote user adoption by demonstrating the value and benefits of reporting and analytics and providing ongoing support and guidance.

7. Regular Review and Improvement: Continuously review and evaluate the effectiveness of reporting and analytics processes. Solicit feedback from users and stakeholders to identify areas for improvement and implement necessary enhancements or modifications.

8. Security and Access Controls: Implement robust security measures to protect sensitive data and ensure appropriate access controls. Define user roles and permissions to restrict data access based on job roles and responsibilities. Regularly review and update security measures to address emerging threats and comply with data privacy regulations.

9. Collaboration and Sharing: Encourage collaboration and sharing of reports and insights across the organization. Foster a culture of data-driven decision-making by promoting knowledge sharing, cross-functional collaboration, and the use of standardized reports and metrics.

10. Continuous Learning and Innovation: Stay updated with the latest trends and advancements in reporting and analytics technologies. Embrace new tools and techniques, such as predictive analytics and machine learning, to enhance the value and capabilities of reporting and analytics in ERP systems.

By following these best practices, organizations can maximize the effectiveness and impact of reporting and analytics in their ERP systems, enabling them to make informed decisions, drive performance improvements, and gain a competitive edge in their industry.

In this chapter, we explored the important components of ERP systems, including the enterprise-wide database, business process automation, integration of functional areas, and reporting and analytics. These components form the backbone of an effective ERP system, enabling organizations to streamline operations, enhance decision-making, and drive growth. In the next chapter, we will dive into the ERP implementation process, covering various stages and discussing the challenges and risks that organizations may encounter during implementation.

6

ERP implementation process

In this chapter, we will delve into the ERP implementation process. We will begin with an introduction to the process and then explore each stage in detail. This includes pre-evaluation screening to identify the right ERP solution, package evaluation to select the most suitable vendor, project planning and management for effective execution, business process mapping and re-engineering to align the ERP system with organizational processes, configuration to tailor the system to specific requirements, testing to ensure functionality and performance, user training for successful adoption, going live to transition to the new system, and post-implementation maintenance to ensure smooth operation. We will also discuss the challenges and risks associated with ERP implementation, such as budget and timeline overruns, resistance to change, data security concerns, organizational culture, data quality issues, change management, and vendor management.

Introduction

The ERP implementation process refers to the series of steps involved in deploying an Enterprise Resource Planning system within an organization. It is a complex and multifaceted undertaking that aims to integrate and streamline various business processes, enhance data management, and improve overall operational efficiency. The implementation process encompasses a range of activities, from initial evaluation and planning to post-implementation maintenance. The ERP implementation process involves pre-evaluation screening, package evaluation, project planning, business process mapping, configuration, testing, user training, going live, and post-implementation maintenance. Pre-evaluation screening assesses the organization's readiness for ERP, while package evaluation selects the suitable ERP software. Project planning outlines the scope, timelines, and resources, while business process mapping optimizes workflows. Configuration customizes the ERP system, testing ensures functionality, and user training imparts skills. Going live marks system deployment, followed by post-implementation maintenance for ongoing support. Challenges include budget and timeline overruns, resistance to change, data security concerns, organizational culture, data quality issues, change management, and vendor management.

Pre-evaluation screening

Pre-evaluation screening is a crucial phase in the implementation of an Enterprise Resource Planning (ERP) system. It involves a comprehensive assessment to determine the organization's readiness for ERP implementation and to gather essential information for making informed decisions. This process includes following points, evaluating various aspects of the organization's current state and setting the foundation for a successful ERP implementation.

1. **Assessing organizational readiness for ERP implementation:**

One key aspect of pre-evaluation screening is assessing the organization's readiness for ERP implementation. This involves evaluating factors such as the organization's strategic alignment with ERP goals, management's commitment and support, and the level of employee readiness and willingness to embrace change. By assessing these factors, organizations can identify any potential barriers or challenges that may impact the success of the implementation and develop strategies to address them.

2. Evaluating current systems and processes:

Another critical component is evaluating the current systems and processes within the organization. This evaluation helps identify strengths, weaknesses, redundancies, inefficiencies, and gaps that may be addressed by implementing an ERP system. By understanding the limitations and opportunities within the existing systems, organizations can determine the specific areas where an ERP solution can bring the most significant benefits and improvements.

3. Identifying the need and potential benefits:

Identifying the need and potential benefits of implementing an ERP system is another essential consideration in the pre-evaluation screening process. Organizations analyze their pain points, challenges, and areas where an ERP system can offer solutions. This evaluation enables organizations to define clear goals, objectives, and desired outcomes for the ERP implementation, aligning the project with the organization's overall strategic direction.

4. Analyzing the scope and scale:

Analyzing the scope and scale of the ERP implementation is crucial to determine the breadth and depth of the project. Organizations assess which functional areas and processes will be included in the ERP system, considering the size of the organization, number of users, and complexity of operations. This analysis helps organizations develop a clear understanding of the project's scope and ensures that all necessary components are considered during the implementation.

5. Determining the resources and budget required:

Determining the necessary resources and budget is another critical aspect of pre-evaluation screening. Organizations assess the human, financial, and technological resources required for a successful ERP implementation. This includes identifying the personnel, hardware, software, and infrastructure needed to support the implementation and ongoing operations. By accurately determining the resources required, organizations can allocate the necessary budget and ensure a smooth implementation process.

6. Conducting a cost-benefit analysis:

Conducting a cost-benefit analysis is an integral part of pre-evaluation screening. Organizations evaluate the costs associated with implementing an ERP system, including initial investment, maintenance, and operational expenses. Simultaneously, organizations quantify the potential benefits that an ERP system can bring, such as improved operational efficiency, streamlined processes, enhanced data visibility, and better decision-making capabilities. By weighing the costs against the expected benefits, organizations can assess the financial viability and feasibility of the ERP project.

7. Assessing the readiness of the organization's infrastructure and technology:

Assessing the readiness of the organization's infrastructure and technology is essential to ensure a smooth ERP implementation.

This evaluation involves analyzing the current IT infrastructure and technology capabilities, identifying any gaps or requirements for hardware, software, network, and data storage. By ensuring that the organization's infrastructure is compatible with the ERP system and can support future scalability and growth, organizations can minimize disruptions and optimize the system's performance.

8. Identifying potential risks and challenges:

Identifying potential risks and challenges is a critical consideration during pre-evaluation screening. Organizations assess various factors that may pose risks to the ERP implementation, such as data security concerns, system integration complexities, and potential disruptions to business operations. By identifying these risks in advance, organizations can develop strategies to mitigate them and minimize the impact on the project's success.

9. Impact on employees and stakeholders:

Considering the impact on employees and stakeholders is another crucial aspect of pre-evaluation screening. Organizations analyze how the ERP implementation will affect employees, including changes to roles, responsibilities, and workflows. It is vital to identify training and support needs to ensure successful adoption and usage of the ERP system. Additionally, organizations consider the impact on other stakeholders, such as customers, suppliers, and partners, and address their concerns and requirements to ensure a smooth transition and continued collaboration.

10. Input and feedback from key stakeholders:

Gathering input and feedback from key stakeholders is an integral part of the pre-evaluation screening process. Engaging management, department heads, and end-users through interviews, surveys, or workshops allows organizations to gather their perspectives, expectations, concerns, and requirements. Incorporating this input and feedback into the evaluation process ensures that the ERP implementation is aligned with the needs and expectations of stakeholders, increasing the likelihood of their buy-in and support.

11. Gap analysis:

Gap analysis is a key component of the pre-evaluation screening process in ERP implementation. It is typically performed during the evaluation of current systems and processes. Gap analysis involves comparing the existing state of the organization's systems and processes with the desired future state enabled by the ERP system. By identifying the gaps or discrepancies between the current and desired states, organizations can understand the areas that need improvement and the specific functionalities that the ERP system should address. Gap analysis helps in defining the scope of the ERP implementation, determining the necessary customization or configuration requirements, and setting realistic expectations for the project. It provides valuable insights into the specific areas where the organization needs to focus its efforts during the implementation process.

12. Pre-evaluation screening report:

The pre-evaluation screening process culminates in the development of a comprehensive report. This report summarizes the findings, assessments, and recommendations resulting from the evaluation. It encompasses the organization's readiness assessment, current system evaluation, identified needs and potential benefits, goals and objectives, scope and scale analysis, resource and budget requirements, risk assessment, and stakeholder input. The pre-evaluation screening report serves as a valuable resource for decision-makers and provides a roadmap for the subsequent stages of the ERP implementation process.

Pre-evaluation screening is a critical phase in the ERP implementation process, enabling organizations to assess their readiness, evaluate current systems, identify needs and potential benefits, and define goals and objectives. Through thorough analysis and evaluation, organizations can make informed decisions, allocate resources effectively, and address potential risks and challenges. The insights gathered during pre-evaluation screening lay the groundwork for a successful ERP implementation, setting the stage for improved efficiency, productivity, and overall business performance.

ERP Package evaluation

ERP package evaluation is a crucial phase in the implementation process where organizations assess and compare different ERP solutions to determine the most suitable one for their needs. This involves considering various factors and conducting thorough research to make an informed decision. The process typically includes defining evaluation criteria, researching available options, preparing a request for proposal (RFP), arranging vendor demonstrations, conducting functional and technical fit analyses, analyzing the total cost of ownership (TCO), assessing vendor viability and support, checking references, and finalizing the selection through contract negotiation. The goal is to choose an ERP package that aligns with the organization's requirements, offers the necessary functionality and scalability, integrates well with existing systems, is financially viable, and is supported by a reliable vendor.

During the ERP package evaluation phase, the following points should be covered:

1. Defining evaluation criteria: Determine the key factors and requirements that the ERP package must meet, such as functionality, scalability, ease of use, industry-specific features, and integration capabilities.
2. Researching available options: Conduct a thorough market research to identify potential ERP vendors and their offerings. Consider factors such as vendor reputation, experience, customer reviews, and market presence.
3. Request for Proposal (RFP): Prepare an RFP document outlining the organization's requirements and send it to selected ERP vendors. This will help gather detailed information about their solutions, pricing, implementation processes, and support services.
4. Vendor demonstrations: Arrange demonstrations with shortlisted vendors to get a firsthand look at their ERP software. This allows stakeholders to assess the system's usability, features, and functionality.
5. Functional fit analysis: Evaluate the ERP package's alignment with the organization's specific functional requirements. Assess how well the system supports core business processes, workflows, and industry-specific needs.
6. Technical fit analysis: Assess the technical compatibility of the ERP package with the organization's existing IT infrastructure. Consider factors such as hardware and software requirements, database compatibility, and integration capabilities.
7. Total cost of ownership (TCO) analysis: Evaluate the overall cost of implementing and maintaining the ERP package over its lifecycle. Consider initial licensing costs, customization expenses, ongoing maintenance and support fees, and potential hidden costs.

8. Vendor viability and support: Assess the financial stability and reputation of the ERP vendors. Evaluate their track record in delivering successful implementations, customer support capabilities, and future development plans.
9. Reference checks: Contact existing customers of the shortlisted ERP vendors to gather feedback on their experiences. This provides valuable insights into the vendor's performance, customer satisfaction, and ability to meet commitments.
10. Final selection and contract negotiation: Based on the evaluation, select the most suitable ERP package and vendor. Negotiate contract terms, pricing, implementation timelines, and support agreements.
11. Final decision approval: Obtain final approval from key stakeholders, such as management and executive sponsors, before moving forward with the chosen ERP package.

By carefully evaluating ERP packages, organizations can ensure they make the right choice for a successful implementation.

Project planning and management

Project planning and management play a crucial role in the successful implementation of an ERP system. To ensure a smooth and effective process, organizations need to address various aspects:

Firstly, it is essential to define the project objectives and scope clearly. This involves outlining the goals, objectives, and desired outcomes of the ERP implementation. Determining the scope of the project is also crucial, identifying the functional areas and processes that will be included.

Next, a comprehensive project plan needs to be developed. This plan serves as a roadmap for the implementation, outlining timelines, milestones, and deliverables. It also involves allocating resources, defining roles and responsibilities, and establishing communication and reporting mechanisms. A well-structured project plan provides clarity and guidance throughout the implementation process.

Identifying and managing project risks is another critical aspect of project planning and management. It involves assessing potential risks and challenges that may arise during the implementation. By developing risk mitigation strategies and contingency plans, organizations can effectively address these risks and minimize their impact on the project.

Effective resource allocation is vital for project success. Organizations need to determine the resources required for the implementation, including personnel, hardware, software, and infrastructure. It is important to ensure that resources are allocated appropriately and in a timely manner to support the project's objectives.

Establishing a project governance structure is essential for effective project management. This involves defining a clear governance framework with roles and responsibilities for project oversight and decision-making. Regular project meetings and reporting mechanisms should be established to monitor progress, address issues, and ensure accountability.

Implementing change management strategies is crucial to navigate the human aspect of ERP implementation. Recognizing the impact on employees and stakeholders, organizations should develop strategies to address resistance to change. This includes providing training and support, facilitating effective communication, and involving stakeholders throughout the project.

Monitoring and controlling project progress is essential to stay on track. Organizations should implement mechanisms to monitor and track progress against established timelines and milestones. Regular reviews should be conducted to assess progress, identify potential issues, and make necessary adjustments to keep the project on schedule.

Effective vendor management is important when working with external ERP vendors. Clear communication channels should be established, expectations managed, and vendor performance monitored throughout the project to ensure a successful partnership.

Engaging stakeholders is crucial for project success. Regularly involving key stakeholders, such as management, department heads, and end-users, helps gather input, address concerns, and keep them informed of project progress and decisions.

Project reviews and evaluations should be conducted periodically. These reviews assess progress, identify areas for improvement, and evaluate the project's success against defined objectives and outcomes. Lessons learned from these evaluations can inform future projects and contribute to continuous improvement.

By addressing these aspects of project planning and management, organizations can establish a solid foundation for their ERP implementation projects, increasing the likelihood of success and achieving their desired outcomes.

Business process mapping and re-engineering

When it comes to business process mapping and re-engineering in the context of ERP implementation, there are several important aspects to consider. Firstly, it is crucial to gain a comprehensive understanding of the current business processes within the organization, including their strengths, weaknesses, and areas for improvement. This involves documenting the existing processes in detail, capturing key information such as inputs, outputs, decision points, and dependencies.

The next step is to identify process improvement opportunities by analyzing the documented as-is processes. This analysis helps in pinpointing areas that can be streamlined, automated, or optimized to enhance overall efficiency. With these insights, organizations can then define the desired future-state processes that align with the capabilities of the chosen ERP system. Best practices, industry standards, and organizational goals are taken into account during the re-engineering process.

Mapping the processes to the functionalities offered by the ERP system is another critical step. This ensures that the ERP system can support and enable the desired future-state processes effectively. It involves identifying how each module, feature, or functionality of the ERP system aligns with specific steps within the processes. Additionally, it is important to assess the impact of process changes and identify any dependencies with other areas of the organization. This evaluation helps in understanding the implications of the changes on other departments, systems, and stakeholders.

To ensure the success of business process mapping and re-engineering, it is essential to engage key stakeholders throughout the process. This includes process owners, subject matter experts, and end-users. Their input and feedback are invaluable for validating process designs, addressing concerns, and ensuring that the changes are embraced by the organization. The future-state processes need to be documented comprehensively, including any modifications made to align with the ERP system.

Implementation plans should be developed to facilitate a smooth transition from the current processes to the new ones. These plans outline the necessary activities such as training, data migration, system configuration, and change management to support the implementation. Once the new processes are in place, continuous monitoring and refinement are vital. Organizations should closely monitor the effectiveness of the implemented processes, gather feedback from users, and make necessary adjustments to optimize performance and drive continuous improvement.

By taking these steps, organizations can effectively map and re-engineer their business processes to align with the capabilities of the ERP system. This optimization of processes leads to improved efficiency, streamlined operations, and maximized benefits from the ERP implementation.

Configuration

During the configuration phase of ERP implementation, several key aspects need to be addressed to tailor the system according to the organization's specific requirements. First, data structures must be defined to determine the types of information that will be stored in the ERP system, such as customer data, product details, and financial records. Workflows within the organization should be carefully analyzed and customized to align with the ERP system, ensuring that the software supports and enhances existing operational processes.

User roles and permissions need to be established to maintain data security and restrict access to sensitive information. By defining user roles and assigning appropriate permissions, organizations can ensure that employees have the necessary access levels based on their job responsibilities. System parameters, such as default values and validation rules, must be set to reflect the organization's preferences and requirements.

Customization of reports and dashboards is essential to provide meaningful and actionable insights to decision-makers at different levels within the organization. By configuring reports and dashboards that present relevant information in a clear and concise manner, organizations can enhance their ability to make informed decisions. Integration with external systems, such as CRM or supply chain management platforms, should be implemented to facilitate seamless data exchange and streamline processes.

Approval workflows need to be defined within the ERP system to establish appropriate authorization processes for critical transactions. By setting up approval workflows, organizations can ensure that necessary validations and authorizations are in place, maintaining control over key business processes. Customization of forms and templates is also important to adapt standard templates within the ERP system to match the organization's branding, layout, and data requirements.

Taxation and compliance rules should be configured to align the ERP system with the specific tax regulations, compliance requirements, and industry standards applicable to the organization's operations. By ensuring compliance within the system, organizations can avoid potential penalties or legal issues. Thorough testing and validation of the configurations are crucial to ensure that the system functions correctly and accurately captures and processes data according to the organization's requirements.

By addressing these aspects during the configuration phase, organizations can optimize the ERP system to fit their specific needs, streamline processes, enhance data accuracy, and improve overall operational efficiency.

Testing

During the testing phase of ERP implementation, several essential activities are undertaken to ensure the system's quality and reliability. Test planning and strategy development form the initial steps, where a comprehensive plan is crafted to outline the objectives, scope, and approach of the testing process.

Test scenarios and test cases are then created to cover various aspects of the ERP system's functionality, providing specific conditions and steps to be executed during testing. Functional testing is conducted to validate the individual components of the system, ensuring they perform as intended. Performance testing assesses the system's ability to handle different workloads, ensuring it can handle the expected volume of data and transactions effectively.

Security testing is performed to identify vulnerabilities and ensure that adequate measures are in place to protect data and the system from unauthorized access. Integration testing verifies the smooth exchange of data between different modules and external systems, ensuring seamless integration and data consistency. User acceptance testing involves end-users to validate the system's usability and effectiveness in real-world scenarios, providing valuable feedback for improvements.

Regression testing is carried out to ensure that system changes or updates do not adversely impact existing functionalities. Defect tracking and management processes are established to identify and address any issues or bugs that arise during testing. Finally, comprehensive documentation and reporting of test cases, results, and encountered issues are maintained to provide valuable references for analysis and reporting to stakeholders.

User training

When it comes to user training for ERP implementation, several key aspects need to be considered. First, it is crucial to assess the training needs of end-users, taking into account their roles and responsibilities within the ERP system. This assessment helps identify the specific knowledge and skills they require to effectively utilize the system. Based on these needs, comprehensive training materials, such as user manuals, job aids, and interactive tutorials, should be developed to support the learning process.

Designing a well-structured training program is also essential. The program should include a combination of theoretical knowledge and practical exercises to ensure users develop a deep understanding of the ERP system. To accommodate different learning styles and preferences, training can be delivered through various methods, such as classroom sessions, online modules, webinars, or a blended approach. It is important to tailor the training content and delivery methods to suit different user groups, such as administrators, managers, and frontline employees, based on their specific needs and level of interaction with the system.

Hands-on training sessions and workshops play a vital role in user training. These sessions provide users with the opportunity to actively navigate the ERP system, perform tasks, and practice using different features and functionalities. System demonstrations can also be conducted to showcase key features and workflows, enabling users to visualize how the system functions and how it can support their daily tasks.

Evaluating the effectiveness of the training program is crucial to ensure its success. Assessments and evaluations should be conducted to gauge user understanding and gather feedback. This feedback helps identify areas for improvement and allows for necessary adjustments to the training approach.

Ongoing support and resources are important for users post-training. Providing access to help desks, user forums, and additional resources such as training videos, FAQs, and reference materials can further enhance users' ability to utilize the ERP system effectively.

By addressing these key points, organizations can ensure that users receive comprehensive and tailored training, empowering them to leverage the ERP system's capabilities and contribute to the success of the implementation.

Going live

The "Going live" phase marks a significant milestone in the ERP implementation process. It involves careful planning and coordination to ensure a smooth transition to the production environment. The following points cover the key aspects of going live:

Firstly, a go-live date is determined, taking into account factors such as project timelines, resource availability, and organizational readiness. This date serves as a target for the deployment of the ERP system.

Next, the production environment is prepared for the deployment. This includes setting up the necessary hardware, software, and infrastructure to support the ERP system. It also involves finalizing the data migration process, ensuring that all required data is accurately transferred to the production environment and validated for integrity.

The cutover plan is executed during the go-live phase. This involves shutting down the old systems, transferring the data to the new ERP system, and starting up the new system. The cutover process is carefully managed to minimize disruptions to business operations and ensure a seamless transition.

System testing is conducted in the production environment to verify the functionality of the ERP system. This includes performing various tests to validate the system's performance, data integrity, and integration with other systems. Any issues or bugs identified during the go-live process are addressed promptly to ensure the system operates effectively.

Throughout the go-live phase, system performance is closely monitored, and user feedback is collected. This helps in identifying any performance issues, usability concerns, or areas for improvement. User support and training are provided to address any questions or challenges that arise, ensuring that employees can effectively use the new ERP system.

The successful go-live is communicated to stakeholders, including employees, management, customers, and partners. This milestone is celebrated as it signifies the completion of the implementation and the beginning of a new phase of operations with the ERP system in place.

Post-implementation (maintenance mode)

The post-implementation phase, also known as the maintenance mode, is a critical stage in the ERP implementation process. It focuses on ensuring the smooth operation and continuous improvement of the ERP system. The following points cover the key aspects of the post-implementation phase:

1. Ongoing Support: Provide ongoing technical support to address any system issues, bugs, or user queries that arise after the implementation. This includes maintaining a

helpdesk or support team to assist users and resolve their concerns.
2. System Monitoring: Continuously monitor the performance and health of the ERP system to identify and address any performance bottlenecks or system issues. This involves implementing monitoring tools and conducting regular system checks.
3. System Upgrades and Patches: Stay updated with the latest releases, upgrades, and patches provided by the ERP vendor. Evaluate the relevance and impact of these updates and apply them to the system to ensure optimal functionality and security.
4. Data Management: Establish processes and procedures for data management, including data backup, data archiving, and data security measures. Regularly review and optimize data storage, integrity, and accessibility.
5. User Training and Education: Provide ongoing training and education to users to enhance their skills and knowledge of the ERP system. This ensures that they can fully leverage the system's capabilities and perform their tasks efficiently.
6. Performance Optimization: Continuously analyze system performance and identify opportunities for optimization. This may involve fine-tuning system configurations, revising workflows, or implementing system enhancements to improve efficiency and user experience.
7. Change Management: Implement change management practices to effectively manage any changes or updates to the ERP system. This includes communicating changes to users, providing training and support during transitions, and ensuring smooth adoption of new functionalities.
8. Stakeholder Engagement: Regularly engage with stakeholders, including employees, management, and end-

users, to gather feedback, address concerns, and identify areas for improvement. This helps in ensuring user satisfaction and aligning the system with evolving business needs.
9. Continuous Improvement: Establish a process for gathering and analyzing system performance data, user feedback, and business requirements to identify areas for continuous improvement. This may involve implementing new features, addressing pain points, or streamlining processes.
10. Documentation and Knowledge Management: Maintain updated documentation of the ERP system, including user manuals, process guidelines, and system configurations. This helps in knowledge sharing, troubleshooting, and training new users.

By focusing on these aspects in the post-implementation phase, organizations can ensure the effective operation, support, and ongoing enhancement of their ERP system to meet their evolving business needs.

Challenges and risks of ERP implementation

Implementing an ERP system can bring numerous benefits to an organization, such as improved efficiency, streamlined processes, and better decision-making. ERP implementation also poses various challenges and risks that organizations need to navigate carefully. These challenges can range from budget and timeline overruns to resistance to change and data security concerns. It is essential for organizations to proactively identify and address these challenges to ensure a successful ERP implementation.

In the following section, we will explore key points that highlight the challenges and risks associated with ERP implementation:

1. Budget and timeline overruns

Budget and timeline overruns are common challenges that organizations may encounter during ERP implementation. These occur when the actual expenditure or time required exceeds the initially estimated or planned amounts. Budget overruns can result from various factors such as underestimated costs, unexpected expenses, scope changes, or inadequate financial planning. Similarly, timeline overruns occur when the project takes longer than anticipated to complete, often due to delays in various phases of implementation, resource constraints, or unforeseen complications. These overruns can have significant implications for the project's success, impacting financial resources, stakeholder satisfaction, and overall project schedule. It is crucial for organizations to carefully monitor and manage their budgets and timelines, employing effective project management techniques, regular tracking of expenses, proactive risk management, and timely decision-making to mitigate the risks associated with budget and timeline overruns.

2. Resistance to change

Resistance to change is a common challenge that organizations face during ERP implementation. It refers to the reluctance or opposition exhibited by individuals or groups within the organization to adopt new processes, systems, or ways of working. People naturally tend to resist change due to various reasons, such as fear of the unknown, loss of familiarity, concerns about job security, and the perception that the change may disrupt existing routines or roles. Resistance to change can manifest in different ways, including lack of enthusiasm, skepticism, passive resistance, or even active sabotage. To address this challenge, organizations need to focus on change management strategies that effectively engage and involve employees throughout the implementation process. This includes fostering open communication, providing clear and compelling reasons for the change, offering training and support to build the necessary skills and knowledge, and involving employees in decision-making and problem-solving. By addressing resistance to change, organizations can help facilitate a smoother transition and increase the likelihood of successful ERP implementation.

3. Data security and privacy concerns

Data security and privacy concerns are critical factors that organizations must address during ERP implementation. With the centralization of data in an ERP system, there is an increased risk of unauthorized access, data breaches, and privacy violations. Organizations need to ensure that robust security measures are in place to protect sensitive and confidential information from external threats as well as internal vulnerabilities. This includes implementing secure authentication mechanisms, encryption protocols, access controls, and regular security audits. Compliance with relevant data protection regulations, such as GDPR or HIPAA, is also crucial to safeguarding customer and employee data. Additionally, organizations should establish clear data governance policies and procedures to define roles and responsibilities, data access privileges, and data retention guidelines. User awareness and training programs can further promote a culture of data security and privacy within the organization. By addressing these concerns proactively, organizations can build trust, maintain data integrity, and mitigate the risks associated with data breaches and privacy violations in the context of ERP implementation.

4. Organizational culture

Organizational culture plays a significant role in the success of ERP implementation. It refers to the shared values, beliefs, norms, and behaviors that shape how work is conducted within an organization. ERP implementation often requires changes to existing processes, workflows, and roles, which can disrupt established routines and challenge the existing organizational culture. Resistance to change, lack of buy-in from employees, and cultural clashes can hinder the smooth adoption and integration of the ERP system.

To address organizational culture challenges, it is important for organizations to foster a culture that embraces change, innovation, and continuous improvement. This can be achieved through effective change management strategies, such as clear and open communication, involvement of employees in decision-making, and providing training and support to facilitate the transition. Organizations should also identify and leverage cultural strengths that align with the goals of ERP implementation, such as a focus on collaboration, adaptability, or customer-centricity. By addressing the cultural aspects and creating an environment that supports the change, organizations can promote acceptance, engagement, and a positive mindset among employees, leading to a smoother and more successful ERP implementation.

5. Data quality issues

Data quality issues can pose significant challenges during ERP implementation. ERP systems rely heavily on accurate and reliable data to perform their functions effectively. However, many organizations face data quality issues, such as incomplete, inconsistent, or outdated data, as well as data duplication or errors. These issues can impact the functionality and efficiency of the ERP system and hinder the organization's ability to make informed decisions based on reliable data.

Addressing data quality issues requires a systematic approach. It involves identifying the root causes of data quality problems, such as inadequate data governance, lack of data standards, or poor data entry practices. Organizations need to establish data governance frameworks and policies to ensure data integrity, accuracy, and consistency. This includes defining data standards, implementing data validation and cleansing processes, and providing training and support to employees responsible for data entry.

Data migration, which involves transferring data from legacy systems to the new ERP system, also requires careful planning and execution to ensure data accuracy and completeness. Data mapping, validation, and testing are essential steps in this process. Organizations should invest time and resources in data cleansing, deduplication, and verification to enhance data quality before migration.

By addressing data quality issues proactively, organizations can improve the reliability and usability of data within the ERP system. This, in turn, enhances decision-making capabilities, enables better operational efficiency, and maximizes the benefits derived from the ERP implementation.

6. Change management

Change management plays a vital role in the successful implementation of an ERP system. It involves managing the transition from the current state to the desired future state, encompassing the changes in processes, systems, and people within an organization. ERP implementation brings significant changes that affect employees' roles, responsibilities, workflows, and mindset. Effective change management strategies are essential to address resistance, increase adoption, and ensure a smooth transition. Communication is a key component, involving transparent and timely dissemination of information about the ERP implementation, its benefits, and the reasons behind the change. Engaging employees early in the process, involving them in decision-making, and addressing their concerns and feedback helps build a sense of ownership and buy-in.

Training and development programs are crucial to equip employees with the necessary skills and knowledge to use the new ERP system effectively. This includes comprehensive training sessions, user manuals, and ongoing support to address any challenges or questions that arise during the transition. Involving stakeholders, such as managers, team leaders, and employees, throughout the change process fosters collaboration and ensures that their perspectives and needs are considered. Change champions or change agents can also be identified within the organization to advocate for the ERP system, provide guidance, and help overcome resistance.

Change management also requires evaluating and adjusting organizational structures, processes, and performance metrics to align with the ERP system. This involves reviewing and redesigning workflows, job roles, and responsibilities to optimize efficiency and effectiveness. By implementing effective change management strategies, organizations can mitigate resistance, enhance employee acceptance and engagement, and facilitate a successful ERP implementation. This ultimately leads to improved organizational performance and the realization of desired benefits from the ERP system.

7. Vendor management

Vendor management is a crucial aspect of ERP implementation that focuses on effectively managing relationships with software vendors and service providers. Selecting the right vendor is essential as they play a significant role in the success of the ERP project. Here are key points to consider in vendor management:

A. Vendor Selection: The process of evaluating and selecting the most suitable ERP software vendor based on factors such as product capabilities, industry expertise, reputation, customer support, and pricing.

B. Contract Negotiation: Negotiating and finalizing the contract terms and conditions with the selected vendor, including licensing, maintenance, support, and service-level agreements.

C. Vendor Relationship: Establishing and maintaining a positive working relationship with the vendor throughout the implementation process and beyond. This involves regular communication, collaboration, and addressing any issues or concerns that arise.

D. Project Management: Collaborating with the vendor to define project goals, timelines, deliverables, and resource requirements. Ensuring that the vendor aligns with the organization's project management approach and methodology.

E. endor Performance: Monitoring and evaluating the vendor's performance against agreed-upon service levels, quality standards, and contractual obligations. Addressing any performance issues promptly to ensure project success.

F. Change Control: Managing changes requested by the vendor, ensuring that they align with the organization's requirements and do not negatively impact project timelines, scope, or budget. Implementing a structured change control process to assess and approve vendor-driven changes.

G. Issue Resolution: Collaborating with the vendor to address any issues, bugs, or system errors that arise during the implementation process. Escalating issues when necessary and working towards timely resolution.

H. Knowledge Transfer: Facilitating knowledge transfer from the vendor to the organization's project team and end-users. This includes training sessions, documentation, and ongoing support to ensure a smooth transition and effective use of the ERP system.

I. Vendor Governance: Establishing a governance framework to manage the vendor relationship and ensure compliance with contractual terms, performance standards, and data security and privacy requirements. This involves regular reviews, performance evaluations, and contract renewals.

Vendor management is crucial for maintaining a productive and collaborative partnership with the ERP vendor, maximizing the value of the implemented system, and addressing any challenges or issues that may arise during and after the implementation process. A well-managed vendor relationship contributes to the overall success and long-term sustainability of the ERP solution.

ERP implementation poses various challenges and risks that organizations must navigate to ensure a successful outcome. By proactively addressing issues such as budget overruns, resistance to change, data security concerns, and organizational culture, organizations can mitigate risks and optimize the benefits of implementing an ERP system.

ERP implementation process is a complex and multifaceted endeavor that requires careful planning, diligent execution, and effective management. From the initial stages of pre-evaluation screening and package evaluation to the final steps of post-implementation maintenance, each phase plays a crucial role in ensuring the successful adoption and utilization of an ERP system. It is important to acknowledge the challenges and risks associated with ERP implementation. By addressing these challenges proactively and employing effective strategies, organizations can overcome obstacles and unlock the transformative potential of ERP systems. With proper planning, commitment, and a focus on continuous improvement, organizations can reap the full benefits of ERP implementation and drive their businesses towards success in the modern digital landscape.

7

Common ERP modules and their functions

This section provides a comprehensive exploration of the various modules within ERP systems. It covers finance, sales and distribution, manufacturing, human resources, plant maintenance, quality management, and materials management modules. The chapter highlights the functions and capabilities of each module, offering readers valuable insights into how they contribute to organizational operations and enhance the efficiency of the ERP system.

Introduction

ERP modules are distinct components or units within an ERP system that handle specific business functions. They are designed to streamline and integrate different aspects of an organization's operations. Some common ERP modules include finance, sales and distribution, manufacturing, human resources, plant maintenance, quality management, and materials management. Each module serves a specific purpose, such as financial accounting, inventory management, production planning, personnel management, equipment maintenance, quality control, and procurement. These modules work together to provide comprehensive support to various functional areas, improving efficiency, data visibility, and decision-making within the organization.

We will now explore ERP modules and their functions.

1. Finance Modules

Finance modules in ERP systems encompass a range of functionalities that are essential for managing financial operations within an organization. These modules are designed to streamline financial processes, ensure accurate recording of financial transactions, and provide insights into the financial health of the company.

One of the key components of finance modules is financial accounting, which involves recording and tracking financial transactions such as revenue, expenses, assets, and liabilities. It enables the generation of financial statements, including balance sheets, income statements, and cash flow statements, providing a comprehensive view of the organization's financial position.

Management accounting is another important aspect of finance modules, focusing on internal financial reporting and analysis. It facilitates budgeting, cost allocation, variance analysis, and performance measurement, allowing managers to make informed decisions based on financial data.

Financial reporting is another function provided by finance modules, enabling the generation of various reports required for regulatory compliance, external audits, and internal reporting purposes. These reports can include financial statements, tax filings, profitability analysis, and financial performance metrics.

Finance modules often offer features for accounts receivable and accounts payable management. This includes invoicing, payment processing, credit management, and vendor management. These functionalities ensure timely and accurate management of customer invoices, payments, and vendor transactions.

They provide a comprehensive suite of tools and functionalities to handle financial accounting, management accounting, financial reporting, and accounts receivable/payable management, enabling organizations to maintain accurate financial records, make informed financial decisions, and comply with regulatory requirements.

2. Sales and Distribution Modules

Sales and distribution modules within ERP systems are designed to streamline and optimize the sales and distribution processes of an organization. These modules provide comprehensive functionalities to manage the entire sales cycle, from order processing to customer relationship management.

At the core of sales and distribution modules is sales order processing, which involves creating and managing customer orders. This includes capturing order details, verifying product availability, determining pricing and discounts, and generating order confirmations. It ensures efficient order management and enables timely order fulfillment.

Pricing and discount management is another crucial aspect of sales and distribution modules. These functionalities allow organizations to define and manage pricing structures, apply discounts, and handle complex pricing scenarios. It ensures accurate and consistent pricing across different customers and products.

Inventory management is an integral part of sales and distribution modules. It enables organizations to track and manage inventory levels, monitor stock availability, and fulfill customer orders based on real-time inventory data. This functionality helps in avoiding stockouts, optimizing inventory levels, and improving order fulfillment efficiency.

Customer relationship management (CRM) features are also present within sales and distribution modules. CRM functionalities provide tools to manage customer information, track interactions, and analyze customer behavior. It helps in building stronger customer relationships, identifying sales opportunities, and providing personalized services to customers.

Sales and distribution modules often include features for managing sales contracts, handling returns and exchanges, and tracking shipments and deliveries. These functionalities ensure effective management of sales agreements, efficient handling of returns, and visibility into the status of shipments.

Sales and distribution modules play a vital role in managing the sales process and maintaining strong customer relationships. They encompass functionalities for sales order processing, pricing and discount management, inventory management, customer relationship management, and related activities. These modules enable organizations to streamline sales operations, enhance customer satisfaction, and drive revenue growth.

3. Manufacturing Modules

Manufacturing modules within ERP systems are specifically designed to support and streamline the manufacturing operations of an organization. These modules encompass a wide range of functionalities to manage different aspects of the manufacturing process, from planning to execution and control.

One key aspect of manufacturing modules is production planning. These modules provide tools to create production plans based on demand forecasts, sales orders, and inventory levels. They help in optimizing production schedules, allocating resources, and ensuring efficient utilization of manufacturing capacities. Production planning functionalities also include features for material requirements planning (MRP), where the system automatically calculates the materials needed for production based on the planned production schedule.

Shop floor control is another critical component of manufacturing modules. These functionalities enable organizations to monitor and manage the activities happening on the shop floor. They provide real-time visibility into production progress, machine utilization, and workforce performance. Shop floor control functionalities help in tracking production orders, capturing actual production data, and addressing any deviations or issues that may arise during the manufacturing process.

Bill of Materials (BOM) management is an essential feature within manufacturing modules. It allows organizations to create and manage the hierarchical structure of products, including the list of components and their relationships. BOM management functionalities help in accurate product costing, inventory management, and production planning. They also facilitate product configuration and versioning, enabling organizations to offer customizable and configurable products to customers.

Quality control is another crucial aspect of manufacturing modules. These functionalities enable organizations to define and enforce quality standards, perform inspections, and track quality-related data. Quality control functionalities help in ensuring product quality, identifying and resolving quality issues, and maintaining compliance with industry regulations and standards.

Manufacturing modules within ERP systems provide comprehensive functionalities to support and optimize the manufacturing operations of an organization. They encompass features for production planning, shop floor control, bill of materials management, and quality control. These modules enable organizations to streamline their manufacturing processes, improve production efficiency, and deliver high-quality products to customers.

4. Human Resources Modules

Human Resources (HR) modules within ERP systems are designed to effectively manage and streamline various HR processes and activities within an organization. These modules encompass a wide range of functionalities to support HR professionals in tasks such as personnel management, time and attendance tracking, payroll processing, and training management.

One key aspect of HR modules is personnel management. These functionalities provide a centralized platform to manage employee information, including personal details, employment history, qualifications, and performance records. HR professionals can easily access and update employee data, track employee assignments and promotions, and maintain a comprehensive employee database. Personnel management functionalities also include features for recruitment and onboarding, allowing organizations to efficiently manage the hiring process and seamlessly integrate new employees into the organization.

Time and attendance tracking is another critical component of HR modules. These functionalities enable organizations to accurately record and manage employee working hours, leaves, and absences. HR professionals can monitor employee attendance, manage leave requests, and generate reports for payroll processing and workforce analysis. Time and attendance tracking functionalities help in ensuring accurate payroll calculations, maintaining compliance with labor regulations, and optimizing workforce scheduling.

Payroll processing is a vital feature within HR modules. These functionalities automate the complex task of calculating employee salaries, taxes, and deductions based on predefined rules and regulations. HR professionals can configure payroll rules, manage salary components, and generate payroll reports for accurate and timely salary disbursement. Payroll processing functionalities also facilitate tax reporting and compliance with statutory requirements, ensuring the organization's adherence to legal obligations.

Training management is another essential aspect of HR modules. These functionalities enable organizations to plan, schedule, and track employee training and development activities. HR professionals can create training programs, manage course catalogs, and track employee participation and progress. Training management functionalities help in enhancing employee skills and competencies, ensuring compliance with training requirements, and fostering a culture of continuous learning and development within the organization.

HR modules within ERP systems provide comprehensive functionalities to support and streamline HR processes within an organization. They encompass features for personnel management, time and attendance tracking, payroll processing, and training management. These modules help HR professionals in effectively managing employee data, tracking working hours and leaves, processing accurate payroll, and facilitating employee training and development. By leveraging HR modules, organizations can optimize HR operations, enhance employee satisfaction, and drive overall organizational success.

5. Plant Maintenance Modules

Plant Maintenance modules in ERP systems are designed to effectively manage and optimize the maintenance activities and processes within an organization. These modules provide a range of functionalities to support plant maintenance professionals in activities such as preventive maintenance, work order management, and equipment tracking.

One crucial aspect of Plant Maintenance modules is preventive maintenance. These functionalities enable organizations to plan and schedule routine maintenance tasks to prevent equipment failures and optimize plant performance. Maintenance professionals can create maintenance schedules, define maintenance plans, and generate work orders for regular inspections, servicing, and repairs. Preventive maintenance functionalities help in reducing downtime, extending equipment lifespan, and maximizing operational efficiency.

Work order management is another essential component of Plant Maintenance modules. These functionalities facilitate the efficient handling of maintenance requests and work orders. Maintenance professionals can receive and prioritize maintenance requests, assign work orders to technicians, and track the progress and completion of maintenance tasks. Work order management functionalities help in streamlining the maintenance workflow, ensuring timely response to maintenance needs, and maintaining proper documentation of maintenance activities.

Equipment tracking is a critical feature within Plant Maintenance modules. These functionalities allow organizations to maintain a comprehensive database of equipment and assets, along with their maintenance history and performance data. Maintenance professionals can track equipment usage, monitor maintenance costs, and schedule equipment inspections and repairs. Equipment tracking functionalities help in optimizing asset utilization, identifying maintenance trends, and ensuring regulatory compliance.

In addition to these core functionalities, Plant Maintenance modules often include features for spare parts management, warranty tracking, and condition-based maintenance. Spare parts management functionalities enable organizations to efficiently manage the inventory of spare parts, track their availability, and facilitate timely replenishment. Warranty tracking functionalities help in monitoring equipment warranties, ensuring timely repairs or replacements under warranty agreements. Condition-based maintenance functionalities leverage real-time data and sensor technology to monitor equipment conditions and trigger maintenance activities based on pre-defined thresholds or indicators.

6. Quality Management Modules

Quality Management modules in ERP systems are designed to ensure the highest level of quality and compliance throughout an organization's processes and operations. These modules provide a wide range of functionalities to support quality planning, inspection, defect tracking, and continuous improvement initiatives.

One of the key functionalities of Quality Management modules is quality planning. These modules enable organizations to define quality standards, establish inspection criteria, and set up quality control parameters. Quality planning functionalities facilitate the creation of quality control plans, including the identification of critical control points, sample sizes, and inspection methods. This ensures that quality requirements are clearly defined and communicated across the organization.

Inspection functionalities within Quality Management modules play a crucial role in monitoring and verifying product and process quality. Organizations can perform inspections at various stages, including incoming goods inspection, in-process inspection, and final product inspection. Inspection results can be recorded and analyzed, allowing for data-driven decisions regarding quality improvement initiatives.

Defect tracking is another important aspect of Quality Management modules. These functionalities enable organizations to identify, record, and track defects or non-conformities throughout the production and supply chain processes. Defects can be categorized, analyzed, and linked to specific products, suppliers, or manufacturing processes. This allows organizations to take appropriate corrective and preventive actions to address the root causes of defects and improve overall quality performance.

Continuous improvement functionalities within Quality Management modules facilitate the implementation of quality improvement initiatives such as Six Sigma, Lean, or Kaizen. These functionalities support initiatives such as corrective actions, preventive actions, and change management. Organizations can identify areas for improvement, initiate corrective actions to address quality issues, and monitor the effectiveness of these actions.

Quality Management modules often include features for document control, calibration management, supplier quality management, and customer complaint handling. Document control functionalities help in managing quality-related documents such as standard operating procedures, work instructions, and quality manuals. Calibration management functionalities facilitate the tracking and scheduling of equipment calibration activities to ensure accurate and reliable measurements. Supplier quality management functionalities enable organizations to assess and monitor the quality performance of suppliers, ensuring that purchased materials and components meet specified quality requirements. Customer complaint handling functionalities support the efficient recording, investigation, and resolution of customer complaints to enhance customer satisfaction and loyalty.

7. Materials Management

Materials Management modules in ERP systems are designed to efficiently manage the flow of materials, from procurement to inventory control to logistics. These modules provide organizations with the tools and functionalities to effectively plan, procure, receive, store, and distribute materials throughout their supply chain.

One of the primary functions of Materials Management modules is procurement management. These modules enable organizations to streamline and automate their procurement processes, from requisition to purchase order creation to vendor selection. Procurement functionalities encompass vendor management, request for quotation, purchase order management, and supplier evaluation. By centralizing and automating procurement activities, organizations can improve sourcing efficiency, negotiate better terms with suppliers, and maintain a reliable supply of materials.

Inventory management is another critical aspect of Materials Management modules. These functionalities allow organizations to monitor and control their inventory levels effectively. Features such as stock valuation, stock categorization, and stock movement tracking enable organizations to optimize inventory levels, reduce carrying costs, and avoid stockouts or overstocking situations. Inventory management functionalities also facilitate inventory replenishment through automated reorder point calculation, material requirements planning (MRP), and just-in-time (JIT) inventory techniques.

Materials Management modules also support the efficient receiving and storage of materials. These functionalities enable organizations to accurately record and track goods receipts, inspect incoming materials for quality and quantity, and manage storage locations and bins. By ensuring proper receiving and storage procedures, organizations can minimize errors, improve inventory accuracy, and enhance overall supply chain efficiency.

Logistics management functionalities within Materials Management modules focus on the transportation and distribution of materials. These features include order fulfillment, shipment planning, delivery scheduling, and route optimization. By optimizing transportation processes and managing delivery schedules, organizations can reduce transportation costs, improve order fulfillment accuracy, and enhance customer satisfaction.

Materials Management modules often integrate with other modules such as finance, sales and distribution, and production planning to provide a holistic view of material-related activities. Integration with finance modules allows for accurate tracking and recording of material costs and financial transactions. Integration with sales and distribution modules ensures seamless order processing and inventory availability for sales orders. Integration with production planning modules facilitates effective material planning and scheduling to support production operations.

Materials Management modules play a crucial role in the effective management of materials within an organization's supply chain. These modules encompass functionalities for procurement management, inventory control, receiving and storage, and logistics management.

This chapter provides a comprehensive exploration of the common ERP modules and their functions. The chapter covers Finance, Sales and Distribution, Manufacturing, Human Resources, Plant Maintenance, Quality Management, and Materials Management modules. It highlights the specific tasks and activities each module is responsible for within an organization's operations. By understanding the functions of these modules, organizations can effectively utilize them to streamline processes, increase efficiency, and make informed decisions.

8

ERP customization and integration

After taking an overview of the essential modules found in ERP systems, including Finance, Sales and Distribution, Manufacturing, Human Resources, Plant Maintenance, Quality Management, and Materials Management in above section this Chapter 8, "ERP customization and integration," delves into the process of customizing ERP systems to align with business requirements and integrating them with other software applications. It discusses the advantages and disadvantages of in-house implementation, the role of vendors and consultants in the customization and integration process, and the importance of involving end-users in the implementation and ongoing usage of the ERP system. The chapter provides insights into the critical considerations and best practices for successfully customizing and integrating ERP solutions to optimize organizational processes and achieve business objectives.

Introduction

ERP customization refers to the process of modifying an ERP system to align with specific business requirements and workflows. It involves tailoring the system's features, functionalities, and interfaces to meet the unique needs of an organization. Customization may involve configuring existing modules, adding new modules, modifying user interfaces, defining workflows, or integrating additional functionalities.

ERP integration, on the other hand, involves connecting the ERP system with other software applications or systems within the organization's technology landscape. Integration enables seamless data exchange and synchronization between the ERP system and other systems, such as CRM, supply chain management, or business intelligence tools. It ensures that information flows efficiently across different departments and systems, eliminating data silos and promoting a unified view of the organization's operations.

The combination of ERP customization and integration enables organizations to maximize the value of their ERP investment by tailoring the system to their specific needs and integrating it into their overall IT ecosystem. This approach allows for streamlined processes, improved data accuracy, enhanced collaboration, and better decision-making capabilities.

ERP customization and integration offer several advantages to organizations, including:

1. Alignment with Business Needs: Customizing an ERP system allows organizations to tailor the software to meet their specific business requirements and workflows. By aligning the system with their unique processes, organizations can optimize efficiency, enhance productivity, and improve overall operational effectiveness.
2. Improved Efficiency and Productivity: Customization enables organizations to streamline processes and eliminate unnecessary steps or modules. This leads to improved efficiency, reduced manual efforts, and increased

productivity. Workflows can be automated, data can be captured and processed more accurately, and employees can focus on value-added activities.

3. Enhanced Decision-Making: Customization and integration facilitate the availability of real-time, accurate, and comprehensive data across different systems. This enables organizations to make informed and data-driven decisions. By integrating ERP with other software applications, organizations can leverage advanced analytics and reporting capabilities, enabling better insights and forecasting.

4. Scalability and Flexibility: Customized ERP systems can easily adapt to changing business needs and growth requirements. Organizations can add or modify functionalities, modules, or interfaces as per their evolving needs, ensuring that the ERP system remains aligned with their current and future business goals.

5. Integration of Systems and Data: ERP integration allows for seamless data exchange and synchronization between the ERP system and other software applications or systems. This integration eliminates data silos, improves data accuracy, and promotes a unified view of the organization's operations. It enables efficient collaboration and facilitates information sharing across different departments.

6. Enhanced Customer Experience: By integrating ERP with customer relationship management (CRM) systems, organizations can gain a holistic view of customer data, interactions, and preferences. This helps in providing personalized customer experiences, improving customer satisfaction, and fostering long-term customer relationships.

7. Cost Savings: Customization and integration help organizations optimize their resources, reduce manual efforts, and eliminate redundant systems or processes. This

can lead to cost savings in terms of time, labor, and operational expenses. Customization and integration reduce the need for multiple standalone systems and their associated maintenance costs.

ERP customization and integration offer organizations the flexibility, efficiency, and scalability to meet their unique business needs, drive operational excellence, and gain a competitive edge in the market.

Customizing ERP to meet business needs

When customizing an ERP system to meet business needs, it is essential to assess the specific requirements of the organization. This involves thoroughly understanding the workflows, processes, and objectives to identify any gaps between the standard functionalities of the ERP system and the business needs. By conducting a comprehensive assessment, organizations can determine the extent of customization required to align the ERP system with their unique requirements.

Customization options are available within ERP systems to tailor various aspects to the organization's needs. This includes customizing workflows and processes to match specific business practices and optimizing the system's functionalities accordingly. Additionally, data customization allows organizations to define and structure data elements to capture and analyze the information that is most relevant to their operations. This ensures that the ERP system can effectively support data-driven decision-making and reporting.

User interface customization is another important aspect of aligning the ERP system with business needs. This involves tailoring the user interface to enhance usability and simplify navigation for end-users. By customizing the user interface, organizations can provide a more intuitive and efficient user experience, resulting in increased productivity and user satisfaction.

Reporting and analytics customization allows organizations to design and generate reports that address their specific reporting requirements. This customization enables the extraction and presentation of relevant data in a format that supports decision-making and facilitates performance monitoring. By customizing reporting and analytics capabilities, organizations can gain deeper insights into their operations and extract meaningful information from the ERP system.

Integration considerations are crucial when customizing an ERP system. Organizations often have existing software applications that need to seamlessly integrate with the ERP system. This requires evaluating integration options, establishing data exchange mechanisms, and ensuring that the ERP system can effectively communicate and share information with other systems. Smooth integration enhances data consistency, improves efficiency, and avoids duplicative efforts.

Before implementing customized changes, thorough testing and validation are necessary to ensure that the customized ERP system operates correctly and meets the intended requirements. Rigorous testing helps identify any potential issues, bugs, or conflicts that may arise from customization. It is crucial to conduct testing in a controlled environment to mitigate risks and ensure the stability and reliability of the ERP system. Documentation and training play a vital role in the successful implementation of customized ERP systems. Comprehensive documentation should be created to capture the customization details, including system configurations, custom workflows, and any changes made to the standard functionalities. This documentation serves as a reference for system administrators, support teams, and end-users.

Training programs should be developed to familiarize users with the customized ERP system and ensure they understand how to effectively utilize the tailored functionalities. Training sessions should cover the new workflows, processes, and features introduced through customization. By providing adequate training and support, organizations can maximize user adoption and optimize the benefits derived from the customized ERP system.

Customizing an ERP system to meet business needs requires a thorough assessment of requirements, identification of gaps, and the selection of appropriate customization options. This includes tailoring workflows, data structures, user interfaces, and reporting capabilities. Integration considerations, testing, documentation, and training are critical elements in ensuring successful implementation and utilization of the customized ERP system. By undertaking customization efforts effectively, organizations can optimize their ERP system to align with their unique business needs and achieve enhanced operational efficiency and effectiveness.

Integrating ERP with other software applications

Integrating an ERP system with other software applications is a critical aspect of leveraging its full potential and achieving seamless data exchange and process optimization across the organization. ERP integration enables different systems to work together harmoniously, ensuring efficient data flow and real-time information access. This integration can span across various areas, such as customer relationship management (CRM), supply chain management (SCM), business intelligence (BI), e-commerce platforms, and more. In this extended note, we will explore the benefits, challenges, and considerations associated with integrating ERP with other software applications.

A. Benefits of ERP Integration:

1. Streamlined Data Flow: Integrating ERP with other software applications eliminates data silos and promotes a centralized data repository. This streamlines the flow of information, reduces manual data entry, and ensures data consistency across systems, leading to enhanced accuracy and productivity.
2. Enhanced Visibility and Reporting: Integration allows real-time data synchronization between systems, enabling comprehensive reporting and analytics. This provides stakeholders with valuable insights, improves decision-making capabilities, and facilitates proactive monitoring of key performance indicators (KPIs) for better business outcomes.
3. Improved Efficiency and Automation: Integration enables automated data exchange and process synchronization, eliminating the need for manual data entry and reducing human errors. This leads to increased efficiency, minimized duplication of efforts, and streamlined operations across the organization.
4. Seamless Collaboration: Integrating ERP with collaboration tools, such as project management systems or communication platforms, fosters seamless collaboration among teams. It enables employees to access and share information in a centralized environment, enhancing teamwork, communication, and productivity.
5. Enhanced Customer Experience: Integration with CRM systems enables a holistic view of customer information,

including purchase history, preferences, and interactions. This empowers organizations to provide personalized services, streamline order processing, and deliver an exceptional customer experience.

B. Challenges and Considerations:

1. Data Compatibility: Integrating ERP with other software applications requires ensuring data compatibility and mapping fields accurately between systems. It is essential to establish data governance practices and define data standards to ensure seamless integration and data consistency.
2. System Complexity: Integrating multiple systems can lead to increased complexity, requiring expertise in integration technologies and APIs. It is crucial to plan the integration architecture, select appropriate integration tools, and involve skilled professionals to handle the technical aspects of integration.
3. Security and Privacy: Integrating ERP with external systems raises security concerns, as sensitive data may be exposed during data exchange. Organizations must implement robust security measures, including data encryption, access controls, and regular security audits, to protect confidential information and comply with data privacy regulations.
4. Change Management: Integration initiatives often require changes in business processes and user workflows. It is important to effectively communicate these changes, provide training and support to end-users, and manage resistance to ensure smooth adoption and utilization of the integrated system.
5. Vendor Collaboration: Successful integration requires collaboration between ERP vendors and other software

application providers. Effective communication, coordination, and shared responsibilities are crucial for ensuring a seamless integration process and resolving any compatibility issues that may arise.

Integrating an ERP system with other software applications offers significant benefits, including streamlined data flow, enhanced visibility and reporting, improved efficiency, seamless collaboration, and enhanced customer experience. By carefully planning, implementing robust integration strategies, and leveraging the expertise of professionals, organizations can unlock the full potential of their ERP system and achieve a connected and optimized technology ecosystem.

In-house Implementation – Pros and Cons

In-house implementation refers to the approach of implementing an ERP system using internal resources and expertise within the organization rather than relying on external consultants or vendors. This approach offers a range of advantages and disadvantages that organizations should consider before deciding on in-house implementation. In this extended note, we will explore the pros and cons of in-house ERP implementation.

A. Pros of In-house Implementation:

1. Cost Control: One of the significant advantages of in-house implementation is cost control. By utilizing internal resources, organizations can potentially save on external consulting fees and vendor charges. This approach allows organizations to allocate their budget towards infrastructure, training, and ongoing support, which can be more cost-effective in the long run.

2. Enhanced Control and Flexibility: In-house implementation provides organizations with greater control over the entire implementation process. They have the flexibility to tailor the implementation approach according to their specific needs, timelines, and priorities. It allows for faster decision-making, customization options, and the ability to adapt the implementation strategy as per the organization's requirements.
3. Knowledge Retention: Implementing ERP in-house allows organizations to build internal knowledge and expertise. The implementation team gains a deep understanding of the system, its functionalities, and the organization's unique requirements. This knowledge retention enables organizations to maintain and enhance the ERP system independently, reducing dependence on external resources in the long term.
4. Organizational Alignment: In-house implementation enables organizations to align the ERP system with their existing processes, workflows, and organizational culture more effectively. Internal teams have a better understanding of the organization's business operations, which can lead to a smoother transition and better integration of the ERP system within the existing structure.

B. Cons of In-house Implementation:

1. Resource and Skill Requirements: In-house implementation demands significant resources in terms of skilled personnel, time, and effort. Organizations need to have a dedicated team with expertise in ERP implementation, project management, technical skills, and change management. Acquiring and retaining such talent

can be a challenge, especially for smaller organizations with limited resources.

2. Implementation Time and Complexity: In-house implementation often requires more time and effort due to the complexities involved. Organizations need to invest in proper planning, system analysis, customization, data migration, and testing. The lack of external expertise may result in a steeper learning curve and potential delays in implementation timelines.

3. Lack of External Perspective: In-house implementation may limit access to external best practices, industry standards, and innovative solutions. Organizations may miss out on the insights and experiences that external consultants and vendors can bring to the table. This could potentially lead to suboptimal system design, configuration, and processes.

4. Support and Maintenance: After the initial implementation, ongoing support and maintenance become the responsibility of the internal team. This can put additional strain on resources, particularly in handling system upgrades, resolving technical issues, and providing user support. Organizations need to ensure they have the necessary expertise and bandwidth to address ongoing maintenance requirements effectively.

5. Risk of Bias and Resistance to Change: In-house implementation may face challenges related to organizational bias and resistance to change. Internal teams may be inclined to prioritize existing processes and resist necessary changes, which can hinder the successful implementation and adoption of the ERP system. Effective change management strategies and strong leadership are

crucial to overcoming resistance and ensuring user acceptance.

In-house implementation offers advantages such as cost control, enhanced control and flexibility, knowledge retention, and organizational alignment. However, organizations must consider the resource and skill requirements, implementation time and complexity, lack of external perspective, support and maintenance responsibilities, and the risk of bias and resistance to change. Careful planning, adequate resources, and a strong commitment to the implementation process are essential to maximize the benefits and overcome the challenges associated with in-house ERP implementation.

Vendors: Role of the Vendor

In ERP implementation, vendors refer to the companies or providers that develop and sell ERP software solutions. These vendors specialize in developing robust ERP systems that cater to the needs of various industries and organizations. They play a crucial role in the implementation process by providing the ERP software, technical expertise, support, and guidance throughout the implementation lifecycle.

Vendors offer a range of services and resources to facilitate successful ERP implementation. Some of the key roles and responsibilities of vendors in ERP implementation include:

1. Software Licensing: Vendors provide organizations with the necessary licenses to use their ERP software. They offer different licensing models, such as perpetual licenses or subscription-based models, allowing organizations to choose the most suitable option based on their needs and budget.

2. System Configuration and Customization: Vendors assist organizations in configuring the ERP system to align with their specific business requirements. They provide tools and resources to customize the software, enabling organizations to tailor workflows, data structures, reports, and user interfaces according to their unique needs.
3. Training and Knowledge Transfer: Vendors offer training programs and resources to educate the implementation team and end-users on how to effectively use the ERP system. They conduct workshops, provide documentation, and offer online resources to ensure that users have the necessary skills to leverage the full potential of the ERP software.
4. Technical Support: Vendors provide technical support to address any issues or challenges that organizations may encounter during the implementation process. They offer help desk services, online forums, and direct assistance to troubleshoot problems, resolve technical issues, and ensure the smooth functioning of the ERP system.
5. Upgrades and Maintenance: Vendors release regular updates and new versions of their ERP software to enhance functionality, address security concerns, and incorporate new features. They provide organizations with access to these upgrades and support organizations in managing the maintenance and upgrade process.
6. Integration and Third-Party Solutions: Vendors assist organizations in integrating the ERP system with other software applications or third-party solutions. They provide tools, APIs, and documentation to enable seamless data exchange and interoperability between the ERP system and other systems used within the organization.
7. Project Management and Consulting: Vendors may offer project management and consulting services to guide

organizations through the implementation process. They provide expertise in ERP implementation methodologies, best practices, and industry-specific requirements, ensuring a structured and successful implementation.

8. Continuous Improvement: Vendors work closely with organizations even after the implementation is complete. They gather feedback, monitor system performance, and collaborate with organizations to identify areas for improvement and provide ongoing support and enhancements to the ERP system.

Vendors in ERP implementation are the companies that develop and provide ERP software solutions. They play a vital role in the implementation process by offering software licenses, system configuration and customization, training and support, upgrades and maintenance, integration services, project management, and continuous improvement. Collaborating with a reliable and experienced vendor can significantly contribute to the success of ERP implementation.

Consultants: Role of Consultants

Consultants in ERP implementation are professionals or consulting firms with expertise in ERP systems and implementation methodologies. They play a critical role in assisting organizations throughout the implementation process, offering specialized knowledge and guidance to ensure a successful ERP deployment. Consultants bring valuable industry experience, technical skills, and best practices to the table, helping organizations streamline their processes, optimize system functionality, and achieve their desired outcomes.

The roles and responsibilities of ERP consultants can vary based on their specific areas of expertise and the needs of the organization. Some common roles and responsibilities of ERP consultants in implementation projects include:

1. Requirements Analysis: Consultants collaborate with key stakeholders to understand the organization's business processes, goals, and challenges. They conduct in-depth analysis and documentation of business requirements, ensuring that the ERP system aligns with the organization's needs.
2. Solution Design: Consultants work closely with the organization's team to design the optimal ERP solution. They utilize their expertise to configure and customize the ERP system, tailoring it to meet the specific requirements and objectives of the organization. They provide recommendations on system architecture, data structures, workflows, and integration with other systems.
3. Project Planning and Management: Consultants play a crucial role in project planning and management. They define project milestones, deliverables, and timelines, ensuring that the implementation stays on track. They allocate resources, manage risks, and communicate project progress to key stakeholders.
4. Business Process Reengineering: Consultants assist organizations in reengineering their business processes to align with the capabilities and best practices supported by the ERP system. They identify inefficiencies, bottlenecks, and areas for improvement, recommending process changes and optimizations to maximize the benefits of the ERP implementation.
5. Data Migration: Consultants guide organizations through the process of migrating data from legacy systems to the new

ERP system. They develop data migration strategies, mapping and transforming data to ensure its accuracy and integrity during the transition. They conduct data cleansing and validation activities to ensure a smooth and successful data migration.

6. Testing and Quality Assurance: Consultants develop comprehensive testing strategies and plans to validate the functionality and performance of the ERP system. They coordinate and execute various testing activities, including unit testing, integration testing, user acceptance testing, and performance testing. They identify and resolve any issues or defects to ensure a high-quality ERP implementation.

7. Training and Change Management: Consultants provide training programs and change management support to help organizations successfully adopt and adapt to the new ERP system. They develop training materials, conduct user training sessions, and provide ongoing support to address user concerns and ensure a smooth transition.

8. Post-Implementation Support: Consultants offer post-implementation support to address any issues or challenges that arise after the ERP system goes live. They provide ongoing assistance, troubleshooting, and guidance to ensure that the system is operating effectively and meeting the organization's expectations.

9. Vendor Management: Consultants may also assist organizations in managing their relationship with ERP vendors. They collaborate with vendors, ensuring that the organization receives the necessary support, updates, and enhancements from the vendor throughout the implementation and beyond.

ERP consultants bring valuable expertise, guidance, and support to organizations during the implementation process. They help organizations navigate the complexities of ERP implementation, optimize system functionality, streamline processes, and maximize the return on investment in the ERP system. Their role is crucial in ensuring a successful and smooth transition to the new ERP environment.

End-Users

End users in ERP implementation are individuals within the organization who will directly interact with the ERP system on a day-to-day basis to perform their job functions. They are the ultimate beneficiaries of the ERP system and play a crucial role in its successful implementation. End users are typically employees from various departments such as finance, sales, manufacturing, human resources, and more, depending on the scope of the ERP system.

A. Importance of End Users:

1. User Adoption: End users are essential for the successful adoption of the ERP system. Their active participation and acceptance of the new system are crucial for realizing the benefits and achieving the desired outcomes of the implementation.
2. System Validation: End users play a vital role in validating the ERP system during the testing phase. They provide valuable feedback, identify any issues or bugs, and help ensure that the system meets their functional requirements and expectations.
3. Process Knowledge: End users possess in-depth knowledge of their respective business processes. Their expertise is invaluable during the implementation, as they can provide insights into process flows, data requirements, and system

functionalities, helping to align the ERP system with the organization's specific needs.

B. Roles and Responsibilities of End Users:

1. Requirements Gathering: End users actively participate in the requirements gathering process. They collaborate with the implementation team to articulate their business needs, specify functional requirements, and define workflows that will be incorporated into the ERP system.
2. User Acceptance Testing: End users are responsible for conducting user acceptance testing (UAT) to validate the ERP system's functionality. They execute test scenarios, identify any discrepancies or issues, and provide feedback to the implementation team for resolution.
3. Training and Knowledge Transfer: End users receive training on how to effectively use the ERP system. They attend training sessions conducted by the implementation team and become familiar with system navigation, data entry, reporting, and other relevant tasks. End users may also serve as trainers or champions within their respective departments to help colleagues adapt to the new system.
4. Change Management: End users play a critical role in change management efforts. They help communicate the benefits of the ERP system to their colleagues, address concerns, and promote the adoption of new processes and workflows. Their involvement in change management activities ensures a smooth transition to the new system.
5. Continuous Improvement: End users provide valuable feedback and suggestions for continuous improvement of the ERP system. They identify areas where the system can be enhanced, provide insights into process efficiencies, and contribute to the ongoing optimization of the system.

6. Data Accuracy and Integrity: End users are responsible for maintaining data accuracy and integrity within the ERP system. They enter and update data as required, ensuring that it remains consistent and reliable for reporting, analysis, and decision-making purposes.

End users are essential stakeholders in ERP implementation. Their active participation, feedback, and commitment to the new system are critical for its success. By embracing the ERP system and effectively utilizing its features, end users contribute to improving business processes, driving operational efficiencies, and achieving the organization's goals and objectives.

This chapter provides a comprehensive exploration of ERP customization and integration. It emphasizes the importance of tailoring ERP systems to meet specific business needs through customization of workflows, processes, data, user interfaces, and reporting capabilities. The chapter also highlights the integration of ERP with other software applications to enhance organizational efficiency. It discusses the pros and cons of in-house implementation, the role of vendors in providing ERP solutions and services, the valuable contributions of consultants in guiding the implementation process, and the significance of end users in validating the system and driving user adoption. By understanding these aspects, organizations can optimize their ERP systems, make informed decisions, and achieve successful business transformation and growth.

9

ERP Market

ERP customization and integration are two important aspects of ERP implementation. Customization allows businesses to tailor ERP systems to meet their specific needs, while integration allows businesses to connect ERP systems with other software applications. Both customization and integration can be complex and time-consuming processes, but they can be worth the effort if they allow businesses to improve their efficiency, productivity, and decision-making.

In Chapter 8 covered ERP customization and integration, including customizing ERP systems, integrating with other software, in-house implementation pros and cons, vendor and consultant roles, and the importance of end-users.

In this Chapter we will explore the ERP market, including an introduction, current state, major vendors and offerings, industry-specific ERP, different business sizes, cloud-based vs on-premise ERP, implementation costs and factors, and future trends.

Introduction to the ERP market

ERP market sets the stage for understanding the landscape and dynamics of this rapidly evolving industry. This chapter provides an overview of the fundamental concepts and context surrounding ERP systems, giving readers a solid foundation to explore the intricacies of the market.

The ERP market is characterized by its size and growth potential. The market has witnessed remarkable expansion, driven by the increasing demand for integrated and automated business solutions. According to market research reports, the ERP market is expected to grow at a substantial rate in the coming years, with significant investments being made by businesses of all sizes to implement and upgrade their ERP systems.

The driving forces behind the adoption of ERP systems are multifaceted. Businesses are recognizing the need for seamless integration and real-time information flow to meet the challenges of a globalized and interconnected world. The digital transformation wave has also played a pivotal role in pushing organizations to embrace ERP systems to stay competitive, improve customer experience, and adapt to evolving market demands.

The ERP market is not a one-size-fits-all scenario. Different industries have specific requirements, and ERP solutions need to cater to their unique needs. Manufacturing, healthcare, retail, and other sectors have their own set of considerations and functionality requirements. For example, manufacturing organizations may require features related to supply chain management, production planning, and inventory control, while healthcare organizations may prioritize patient management, billing, and regulatory compliance.

The ERP market is a large and growing market. The major ERP vendors are SAP, Oracle, Microsoft, and Infor. ERP systems are available for a variety of industries and business sizes. Cloud-based ERP systems are becoming increasingly popular. The cost of implementing ERP systems can vary depending on the size of the business and the complexity of the system. The ERP market is constantly evolving, and new trends are emerging all the time.

The ERP market is witnessing a shift towards cloud-based solutions, with organizations increasingly opting for software-as-a-service (SaaS) models. Cloud-based ERP offers flexibility, scalability, and cost-effectiveness, allowing businesses to access their systems from anywhere at any time. On-premise ERP solutions, on the other hand, provide organizations with more control and customization options but require substantial infrastructure and maintenance investments.

Looking ahead, the ERP market is expected to witness further advancements and trends. Innovations such as artificial intelligence, machine learning, and predictive analytics are being integrated into ERP systems to enable data-driven insights and automation. Mobile accessibility, user-friendly interfaces, and enhanced user experiences are also driving the evolution of ERP solutions

Current state of the ERP market

The current state of the ERP market reflects the ever-growing demand for integrated and efficient business solutions. As organizations strive to streamline their operations, gain insights from data, and enhance collaboration across departments, ERP systems have become an essential tool in achieving these goals.

ERP market is a large and growing market. The global ERP market was valued at $44.47 billion in 2022 and is projected to grow to $71.34 billion by 2030. The growth of the ERP market is being driven by a number of factors, including the increasing demand for enterprise-wide visibility and control, the need to improve efficiency and productivity, and the growing adoption of cloud computing.

One prominent trend in the ERP market is the adoption of cloud-based ERP solutions. Cloud computing has revolutionized the way businesses operate by offering flexibility, scalability, and cost-effectiveness. Cloud-based ERP allows organizations to access their systems and data from anywhere, at any time, through a web browser or mobile application. This flexibility eliminates the need for on-premise infrastructure and reduces maintenance costs. As a result, more and more organizations are migrating from traditional on-premise ERP systems to cloud-based solutions.

Another significant trend is the integration of artificial intelligence (AI) and machine learning (ML) capabilities into ERP systems. AI and ML algorithms can analyze vast amounts of data, identify patterns, and provide actionable insights for decision-making. These technologies automate routine tasks, optimize processes, and enhance predictive capabilities, enabling organizations to make data-driven decisions and improve operational efficiency. AI-driven chatbots and virtual assistants are also being integrated into ERP systems to enhance user experiences and provide personalized support.

The ERP market is also witnessing increased focus on mobile accessibility and user-friendly interfaces. Mobile ERP applications enable employees to access critical business information, collaborate on tasks, and perform transactions on their smartphones or tablets. User-friendly interfaces make ERP systems more intuitive and easier to navigate, reducing training time and improving user adoption. The availability of real-time dashboards, interactive reports, and personalized analytics empowers users to make informed decisions on the go.

Industry-specific ERP solutions are gaining traction in the market. Different industries have unique requirements and regulations that need to be addressed by ERP systems.

Manufacturing, healthcare, retail, construction, and other sectors have specific functionalities and workflows that are tailored to their needs. Industry-specific ERP solutions offer preconfigured modules, templates, and best practices designed to meet the specific requirements of each industry, enabling faster implementation and reducing customization efforts.

The current state of the ERP market also reflects the shift towards a more customer-centric approach. Vendors are focusing on delivering comprehensive solutions that not only address core ERP functionalities but also cater to customer experience, support, and ongoing services. Customer satisfaction and long-term partnerships are critical success factors in the highly competitive ERP market.

In terms of market dynamics, the ERP market is highly competitive, with several major players dominating the landscape. SAP, Oracle, Microsoft, Infor, and Epicor are among the leading ERP vendors with a strong market presence and a wide range of product offerings. These vendors provide ERP solutions for organizations of all sizes and across various industries. They continuously invest in research and development to innovate their offerings and stay ahead of the market demands.

Factors such as cost, scalability, customization options, ease of use, and integration capabilities are important considerations for organizations when selecting an ERP solution. Implementation costs, including software licensing, infrastructure, customization, data migration, and training, are critical factors that organizations need to evaluate. The ability to scale the ERP system as the organization grows and the ease of integrating with other software applications are crucial for long-term success.

Looking ahead, the future of the ERP market is promising. The rapid advancement of technology, including AI, ML, IoT (Internet of Things), and big data analytics, will continue to shape the ERP landscape. These technologies will further enhance automation, data analysis, and decision-making capabilities within ERP systems. The increasing adoption of Industry 4.0 practices, such as smart manufacturing and digital supply chain management, will also drive the demand for advanced ERP solutions.

Major ERP vendors and their offerings

The ERP market is populated by several major vendors who provide comprehensive solutions to organizations of all sizes and industries. These vendors have established themselves as leaders in the ERP industry, offering a wide range of features and functionalities to meet the diverse needs of businesses. Let's delve into the offerings of some of the prominent ERP vendors:

1. SAP India: SAP is the world's largest ERP vendor, with over 400,000 customers in over 180 countries [1]. SAP offers a wide range of ERP solutions, including SAP S/4HANA, SAP Business One, and SAP Business ByDesign. SAP S/4HANA is SAP's flagship ERP solution, and it is designed for large enterprises. SAP Business One is a smaller, more ffordable ERP solution that is designed for small and medium-sized businesses. SAP Business ByDesign is a cloud-based ERP solution that is designed for growing businesses [2].

Figure 4. Major ERP Vendors

2. Oracle India: Oracle offers a wide range of ERP solutions, including Oracle Fusion Cloud ERP, Oracle NetSuite ERP, and Oracle JD Edwards EnterpriseOne. Oracle Fusion Cloud ERP is Oracle's flagship ERP solution, and it is designed for large enterprises. Oracle NetSuite ERP is a cloud-based ERP solution that is designed for small and medium-sized businesses. Oracle JD Edwards EnterpriseOne is a traditional on-premises ERP solution that is designed for large enterprises. Oracle's ERP offerings are highly customizable and provide advanced analytics and reporting capabilities [3].

3. Microsoft India: Microsoft is the third largest ERP vendor in the world. Microsoft offers a wide range of ERP solutions, including Microsoft Dynamics 365 Business Central,

Microsoft Dynamics 365 Finance and Operations, and Microsoft Dynamics 365 Supply Chain Management. Microsoft Dynamics 365 Business Central is a cloud-based ERP solution that is designed for small and medium-sized businesses. Microsoft Dynamics 365 Finance and Operations is a cloud-based ERP solution that is designed for large enterprises [4]. Microsoft Dynamics 365 Supply Chain Management is a cloud-based ERP solution that is designed for supply chain management.

4. Tally Solutions India: Tally Solutions is a well-known Indian ERP vendor that specializes in accounting and financial management software [5]. Tally ERP 9 is their flagship product, widely used by small and medium-sized businesses for managing financial transactions, inventory, payroll, and taxation. Tally ERP 9 offers localization for Indian tax regulations and is popular for its user-friendly interface and ease of use.

5. Ramco Systems: Ramco Systems provides a comprehensive suite of ERP solutions for various industries, including manufacturing, aviation, logistics, and services [6]. Their offerings include Ramco ERP, Ramco HCM, Ramco Logistics, and Ramco Aviation. Ramco ERP covers finance, supply chain management, procurement, manufacturing, and human resources. Their solutions are known for their mobility features, cloud readiness, and focus on specific industries.

6. Infor India: Infor is a leading provider of enterprise software solutions, including ERP, supply chain management, and customer relationship management (CRM). Infor offers a wide range of ERP solutions, including Infor M3, Infor LN, and Infor CloudSuite. Infor M3 is a traditional on-premises ERP solution that is designed for large enterprises [7]. Infor

LN is a traditional on-premises ERP solution that is designed for manufacturing and distribution companies. Infor CloudSuite is a cloud-based ERP solution that is designed for small and medium-sized businesses.

7. QAD India: QAD is a global provider of cloud-based ERP solutions for manufacturing companies. QAD India offers solutions such as QAD Adaptive ERP and QAD Cloud ERP [8]. These solutions address the needs of manufacturers in areas like finance, supply chain management, manufacturing operations, and demand planning. QAD's focus on manufacturing expertise makes it a popular choice for companies in this sector.

8. Focus Softnet: Focus Softnet is an ERP vendor that offers a range of ERP solutions for different industries, including manufacturing, retail, distribution, and services [9]. Their offerings include Focus i, a comprehensive ERP system covering finance, inventory, sales, and human resources. Focus Softnet also provides industry-specific solutions such as Focus RT, Focus WMS, and Focus POS, catering to the unique requirements of different sectors.

9. Epicor: Epicor provides ERP solutions tailored to meet the needs of manufacturing, distribution, retail, and service industries. Their ERP offerings, including Epicor ERP and Prophet 21, offer modules for finance, inventory management, production planning, customer relationship management, and more. Epicor's solutions are known for their scalability, ease of use, and industry-specific capabilities [10].

10. Sage: Sage is a leading provider of business management software solutions, including ERP, accounting, and payroll. Sage offers a wide range of ERP solutions, including Sage 100, Sage 300, and Sage 500. Sage 100 is a traditional on-

premises ERP solution that is designed for small and medium-sized businesses. Sage 300 is a traditional on-premises ERP solution that is designed for mid-sized businesses [11]. Sage 500 is a traditional on-premises ERP solution that is designed for small businesses.

These major ERP vendors continue to innovate and enhance their offerings to stay ahead in the competitive market. They often provide additional services such as implementation support, training, and ongoing customer support. Organizations evaluate these vendors based on factors such as industry fit, scalability, customization options, integration capabilities, total cost of ownership, and long-term strategic alignment.

While Google, Zoho, and custom-made small vendor ERP systems may offer certain ERP-like functionalities, they are not considered comprehensive ERP solutions in the traditional sense. Established ERP vendors often provide more robust and feature-rich offerings designed to address the diverse needs of businesses across various industries.

ERP for different industries

ERP systems have become integral to the operations of various industries, offering comprehensive solutions to streamline processes, improve efficiency, and enhance overall productivity. Let's explore how ERP is tailored to meet the specific needs of different industries, including manufacturing, healthcare, retail, and more.

1. Manufacturing Industry: ERP systems play a crucial role in the manufacturing sector by optimizing production planning, inventory management, and supply chain operations. They facilitate real-time tracking of materials,

enable efficient resource allocation, and provide insights into production costs and quality control. With modules for shop floor control, bill of materials management, and demand forecasting, ERP systems empower manufacturers to enhance productivity, reduce lead times, and ensure effective resource utilization.

2. Healthcare Industry: ERP solutions for the healthcare sector focus on managing patient information, streamlining administrative tasks, and ensuring regulatory compliance. They encompass modules for patient management, electronic health records, scheduling, billing, and inventory control. By centralizing patient data, automating processes, and enabling seamless collaboration between departments, ERP systems enhance the quality of patient care, improve operational efficiency, and support informed decision-making.

3. Retail Industry: ERP systems in the retail industry address key aspects such as inventory management, sales tracking, and customer relationship management. They enable retailers to optimize inventory levels, monitor product demand, and streamline purchasing processes. With integration capabilities for point-of-sale systems, online sales platforms, and customer loyalty programs, ERP systems facilitate a seamless omnichannel retail experience. They provide insights into customer behavior, enable personalized marketing strategies, and enhance customer satisfaction and retention.

4. Service Industry: ERP systems also cater to the unique requirements of the service industry, which includes professional services, consulting firms, and hospitality businesses. These systems facilitate project management, resource allocation, time tracking, and invoicing for service-

based businesses. They enable effective resource utilization, project cost tracking, and accurate billing, ensuring profitability and client satisfaction.
5. Financial Sector: ERP solutions for the financial sector focus on financial management, accounting, and reporting functionalities. They help automate financial processes, consolidate data from various departments, and provide real-time financial insights. These systems support budgeting, expense management, asset tracking, and financial analysis, enabling financial institutions to optimize financial performance, ensure compliance, and make data-driven decisions.

While ERP systems offer industry-specific modules and functionalities, they can also be customized to meet the unique requirements of organizations within each industry. Whether it's manufacturing, healthcare, retail, or any other sector, ERP systems provide a unified platform that streamlines operations, enhances collaboration, and drives business growth. By leveraging the power of ERP, organizations across industries can improve efficiency, make informed decisions, and stay competitive in today's dynamic business landscape.

ERP for different business sizes

ERP systems are designed to cater to the needs of businesses of all sizes, including small, medium, and large enterprises. Let's explore how ERP solutions are tailored to address the specific requirements of each business size category.

1. Small Businesses: ERP systems for small businesses focus on affordability, simplicity, and scalability. These solutions offer essential functionalities such as financial management,

inventory control, sales tracking, and basic reporting capabilities. They are often cloud-based, providing ease of implementation and maintenance while minimizing upfront costs. ERP systems for small businesses enable process automation, centralize data management, and streamline day-to-day operations, allowing small businesses to optimize efficiency and make informed decisions to support their growth and competitiveness.

2. Medium-Sized Businesses: ERP systems for medium-sized businesses provide a broader range of functionalities to support their expanding operations. These solutions typically encompass modules for financial management, supply chain management, human resources, customer relationship management, and more. They offer robust reporting and analytics capabilities, enabling medium-sized businesses to gain better visibility into their operations and make data-driven decisions. ERP systems for medium-sized businesses are designed to handle increased transaction volumes, support multi-site operations, and facilitate collaboration across departments. They provide scalability and flexibility to adapt to changing business needs and regulatory requirements.

3. Large Enterprises: ERP systems for large enterprises are highly comprehensive and tailored to meet complex business requirements. These solutions encompass a wide range of modules, including finance, manufacturing, distribution, human resources, procurement, and more. They offer advanced features such as advanced analytics, enterprise-wide data integration, workflow automation, and extensive customization capabilities. ERP systems for large enterprises enable seamless collaboration across multiple business units and locations, support complex supply chain

operations, and provide deep insights into organizational performance. They are designed to handle large-scale data processing and offer enterprise-level security and governance features.

Regardless of the business size, implementing an ERP system brings several benefits. It enhances operational efficiency, streamlines processes, improves data accuracy, enables better decision-making, and supports growth. ERP systems provide a centralized platform that integrates various business functions, facilitating information flow and enabling a holistic view of the organization. They eliminate silos, reduce manual effort, and promote cross-functional collaboration.

Cloud-based ERP vs On-premise ERP

In the realm of Enterprise Resource Planning (ERP) systems, organizations have the choice between deploying a cloud-based ERP or an on-premise ERP solution. Both options have their own advantages and considerations. Let's delve into a detailed comparison of cloud-based ERP and on-premise ERP to understand their key characteristics and help businesses make an informed decision.

A. Cloud-based ERP:

Cloud-based ERP refers to ERP software that is hosted and managed by a third-party provider on their infrastructure. Here are some key aspects of cloud-based ERP:

1. Accessibility and Scalability: Cloud-based ERP offers the advantage of accessibility from anywhere with an internet connection. Users can access the system and relevant data

through web browsers or mobile apps, enabling remote work and enhancing collaboration. Cloud-based ERP solutions are also highly scalable, allowing businesses to easily adjust their resource usage as needed, whether it's adding or reducing users, modules, or storage capacity.

2. Cost-efficiency: Cloud-based ERP operates on a subscription-based model, where organizations pay a recurring fee for software usage and hosting services. This eliminates the need for significant upfront investments in hardware infrastructure and IT resources. Additionally, the cloud provider handles software updates, maintenance, and backups, reducing the burden on internal IT teams and associated costs.

3. Flexibility and Customization: Cloud-based ERP solutions often provide flexible configurations and customization options to align with specific business needs. Organizations can choose the modules and features they require and customize workflows and processes accordingly. However, it's important to note that extensive customizations may impact the ease of upgrades and future compatibility.

4. Security and Reliability: Cloud-based ERP vendors invest heavily in robust security measures to protect data and ensure compliance with industry standards. They employ encryption, regular backups, disaster recovery plans, and continuous monitoring to mitigate security risks. Additionally, reputable cloud providers offer high levels of reliability and uptime, ensuring minimal disruptions to business operations.

B. **On-premise ERP:**

On-premise ERP involves deploying ERP software on servers and infrastructure located within an organization's premises. Here are some key aspects of on-premise ERP:

1. Control and Customization: On-premise ERP provides organizations with greater control over their systems and data. It allows extensive customization to meet unique business requirements. Companies can tailor the ERP solution to their specific processes and integrate it with other on-premise systems, such as legacy applications or proprietary software.
2. Data Security: With on-premise ERP, organizations retain full control over their data security measures. They can implement internal security protocols and safeguards according to their specific needs and industry regulations. However, ensuring data security requires dedicated resources and expertise from the organization's IT department.
3. Initial Investment and Maintenance: On-premise ERP typically involves higher upfront costs, including hardware infrastructure, licensing fees, implementation, and ongoing maintenance. Organizations need to invest in servers, networking equipment, and IT personnel to manage the system's operations, updates, backups, and security.
4. Scalability and Upgrades: Scalability and upgrades in on-premise ERP require additional investments in hardware and resources. Organizations must plan and execute upgrades carefully to minimize disruptions and ensure compatibility with existing customizations.
5. Choosing the Right Option: When deciding between cloud-based ERP and on-premise ERP, organizations must consider their specific needs, budget, security requirements, industry compliance, scalability, and future growth plans.

Small to mid-sized businesses often find cloud-based ERP more suitable due to its affordability, scalability, and reduced IT burden. Large enterprises with complex operations may prefer the control and customization capabilities of on-premise ERP.

Table 4. Comparison of Cloud-based ERP and On-premise ERP

Factor	Cloud-based ERP	On-premise ERP
Scalability	Easy to scale up or down as needed	More difficult to scale
Cost-effectiveness	Typically more cost-effective	Can be more expensive, especially for large businesses
Ease of use	Typically easier to use	Can be more difficult to use, especially for businesses with complex needs
Security	Typically more secure	Can have more control over security
Customization	Less customizable	More customizable
Uptime	Typically has higher uptime	Can have lower uptime, especially during maintenance
Support	Typically offers online support	May offer phone support or on-site support

Tab. 1 shows factors comparing Cloud-based ERP and On-premise ERP.

In recent years, hybrid ERP solutions that combine elements of both cloud-based and on-premise models have gained popularity. These solutions offer the flexibility to host certain modules or sensitive data on-premise while utilizing cloud-based ERP for other functionalities.

The choice between cloud-based ERP and on-premise ERP depends on a thorough evaluation of organizational requirements, resources, budget, and long-term strategic objectives. Implementing the right ERP solution can empower businesses to streamline operations, enhance productivity, and achieve sustainable growth in today's dynamic business landscape.

Implementation costs and factors affecting them

Implementation costs play a crucial role in determining the feasibility and success of an ERP system in an organization. Several factors influence the implementation costs of ERP systems. It is essential for businesses to consider these factors to accurately assess and plan their budget for ERP implementation.

1. ERP Software License: The cost of ERP software licenses can vary depending on the vendor, functionality, and user licenses required. The pricing structure may be based on the number of users, modules, or concurrent users. It is essential to evaluate different vendors and their pricing models to choose a cost-effective option that aligns with the organization's requirements.
2. Customization and Configuration: Customizing and configuring the ERP system to meet specific business needs often incurs additional costs. This involves tailoring workflows, reports, and interfaces, and can vary based on the complexity of customization required. It is crucial to strike a balance between customization and standard functionality to avoid excessive costs.
3. Hardware and Infrastructure: Implementing an ERP system may require investing in new hardware infrastructure, such as servers, storage devices, networking equipment, and backup systems. The cost of hardware can vary based on the organization's size and scalability requirements. Cloud-

based ERP systems may reduce hardware costs as they rely on remote servers and infrastructure.

4. Implementation Services: Engaging ERP implementation services from consultants or vendors is a significant cost factor. These services include project planning, system configuration, data migration, training, and post-implementation support. The costs can vary based on the complexity of the implementation, the duration of the project, and the expertise of the service provider.
5. Data Migration: Transferring existing data from legacy systems to the new ERP system can involve data cleansing, mapping, and validation processes. The complexity and volume of data can impact the cost of data migration services. It is essential to allocate sufficient resources and budget for this critical task.
6. Training and Change Management: Training end-users and facilitating change management are vital aspects of ERP implementation. Costs associated with training programs, user manuals, workshops, and change management initiatives should be considered. Investing in comprehensive training can enhance user adoption and minimize disruptions during the transition.
7. Ongoing Maintenance and Support: ERP systems require regular maintenance, updates, and support. Vendors often provide maintenance and support services under annual contracts, and the costs may vary based on the level of support required. It is crucial to factor in these recurring costs to ensure continued system performance and support.
8. Organizational Size and Complexity: The size and complexity of the organization can significantly impact implementation costs. Larger organizations with multiple departments, locations, and complex processes may require

more extensive customization, data migration, and training efforts, resulting in higher costs.

9. Project Management: Adequate project management is crucial for a successful ERP implementation. Allocating resources for project management, including project managers and coordinators, can help streamline the implementation process and ensure effective communication and coordination.
10. External Factors: External factors such as currency fluctuations, inflation, and market dynamics can also influence implementation costs. It is important to consider these factors while planning the budget to account for any potential financial impacts.

Implementing an ERP system involves various cost factors that need careful consideration. Organizations should conduct a thorough analysis of their requirements, conduct vendor evaluations, and engage in cost-benefit analysis to determine an accurate budget for ERP implementation. Effective cost management and proper planning can help organizations maximize the value derived from their ERP investment and achieve successful outcomes.

ERP trends and future outlook

ERP trends

ERP is continuously evolving, driven by technological advancements and changing business needs. In the current landscape, several key trends are shaping the future outlook of ERP systems. One prominent trend is the increasing adoption of cloud-based ERP solutions. Organizations are seeking the flexibility, scalability, and cost-effectiveness offered by cloud ERP, allowing them to access their systems from anywhere, enjoy seamless upgrades, and reduce infrastructure requirements.

Another significant trend is the rise of mobile ERP. With the growing use of mobile devices, ERP systems are becoming more mobile-friendly. Mobile ERP apps enable users to access critical data, perform tasks, and make informed decisions on the go, enhancing productivity and efficiency. Furthermore, the integration of Artificial Intelligence (AI) and Machine Learning (ML) technologies into ERP systems is gaining momentum. These technologies automate routine tasks, improve data analysis, and provide intelligent insights, enabling predictive analytics, anomaly detection, and process optimization.

The Internet of Things (IoT) is also playing a crucial role in shaping the future of ERP. IoT devices are being integrated with ERP systems, enabling real-time data collection, monitoring, and analysis. This integration enhances supply chain management, asset tracking, and predictive maintenance capabilities. Blockchain technology is being explored for its potential in ERP systems. It can enhance security, transparency, and traceability in transactions, supply chain visibility, and trusted data sharing across multiple entities.

A focus on user experience (UX) is another key trend in ERP. Vendors are striving to improve the user experience by providing intuitive interfaces, personalized dashboards, and role-based access. User-centric design enhances user adoption and productivity, driving the future direction of ERP systems.

Future outlook

Looking ahead, the future outlook of ERP systems holds exciting possibilities. Intelligent automation will further leverage AI, ML, and robotic process automation (RPA) to automate complex tasks, improve decision-making, and enhance operational efficiency. Advanced analytics capabilities will evolve to provide deeper insights, predictive analysis, and data-driven decision-making. Industry-specific ERP solutions will continue to be developed, catering to the unique needs of various sectors.

Enhanced security measures will be a top priority, with ERP systems incorporating multi-factor authentication, encryption, and real-time threat detection to safeguard sensitive data. Integration with emerging technologies such as augmented reality (AR), virtual reality (VR), and edge computing will enable immersive experiences, remote collaboration, and real-time data processing at the edge.

Sustainability and green ERP solutions will gain importance as organizations strive to address environmental challenges. ERP systems will incorporate features for energy management, waste reduction, and carbon footprint tracking, supporting organizations in achieving their sustainability goals.

Agile and flexible ERP solutions will become prevalent, allowing organizations to quickly adapt to changing business requirements, scale operations, and support remote work models. Embracing these ERP trends and future outlook is crucial for organizations to stay competitive, drive innovation, and achieve digital transformation. By leveraging these advancements, organizations can streamline operations, optimize resources, and unlock new growth opportunities in the dynamic ERP landscape.

10

Future of ERP

In this chapter 10, we will focus on the future of ERP, examining emerging technologies, evolving business needs, and their impact on ERP systems. We'll explore advancements in AI, machine learning, IoT, and other trends that will shape the future of ERP and guide organizations in their digital transformation journey.

Introduction

The future of ERP holds great promise as organizations continue to embrace digital transformation and leverage emerging technologies to drive innovation and efficiency. With the rapid advancements in artificial intelligence, machine learning, cloud computing, Internet of Things (IoT), and data analytics, ERP systems are evolving to become more intelligent, flexible, and user-centric. The future of ERP will see enhanced automation, predictive capabilities, real-time analytics, seamless integration with other technologies, and personalized user experiences. Organizations can expect ERP systems to empower them with greater agility, improved decision-making, and the ability to adapt to changing business needs. As we explore the future of ERP, we will witness how these advancements revolutionize the way businesses operate, enabling them to stay competitive and thrive in a rapidly evolving digital landscape.

Historical evolution of ERP technology

The historical evolution of ERP technology spans several decades, starting from its roots in Material Requirements Planning (MRP) systems in the 1970s. MRP systems focused on managing inventory and production planning. Over time, the concept evolved into Manufacturing Resource Planning (MRP II) systems in the 1980s, incorporating additional functionalities such as capacity planning, scheduling, and financial management. In the 1990s, Enterprise Resource Planning (ERP) systems emerged, integrating various business functions like finance, sales, procurement, and human resources into a single, centralized system. These early ERP systems were primarily on-premise solutions, requiring substantial investments in hardware and infrastructure.

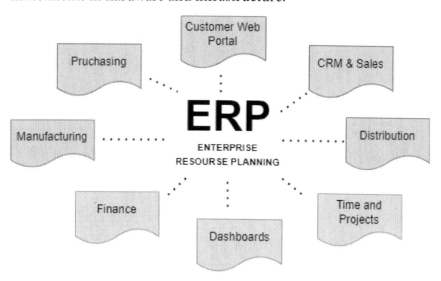

Figure 5. Image showing future of ERP

Current state of the ERP market

The current state of the ERP market is marked by rapid growth and innovation, driven by the increasing demand for integrated and streamlined business management solutions. ERP systems have become an essential tool for organizations across various industries, ranging from small businesses to large enterprises. The market is characterized by a diverse range of ERP vendors, each offering their unique set of features and functionalities. The competition among vendors has led to continuous advancements in ERP technology, resulting in more robust and sophisticated solutions.

One prominent trend in the current ERP market is the shift towards cloud-based ERP systems. Cloud-based ERP offers numerous benefits, including scalability, flexibility, and cost-effectiveness. Organizations can leverage the cloud to access their ERP systems from anywhere, facilitating remote work and enabling seamless collaboration. Cloud-based ERP eliminates the need for upfront hardware investments and reduces maintenance costs, making it an attractive option for businesses of all sizes. As a result, the adoption of cloud-based ERP solutions has been on the rise, and many vendors now offer cloud deployment options alongside traditional on-premise solutions.

Another notable aspect of the current ERP market is the integration of emerging technologies. ERP systems are incorporating technologies like artificial intelligence (AI), machine learning, robotic process automation (RPA), and analytics to enhance functionality and provide intelligent insights. AI and machine learning capabilities enable automation, predictive analysis, and intelligent decision-making, improving operational efficiency and driving business growth. Furthermore, ERP systems are integrating with IoT devices to gather real-time data from various sources, enabling organizations to optimize processes and improve decision-making based on actionable insights. The current state of the ERP market reflects a dynamic and evolving landscape, with vendors continuously innovating to meet the evolving needs of businesses in the digital era.

Emerging trends in ERP technology

ERP systems have been around for decades, but they are constantly evolving to meet the needs of businesses in the digital age.

In recent years, there has been a number of emerging trends in ERP technology. These trends are shaping the future of ERP and will have a significant impact on businesses of all sizes.

Some of the key emerging trends in ERP technology include:

1. Artificial Intelligence (AI) and Machine Learning (ML)

Emerging trends in ERP technology are revolutionizing the way businesses operate, and two of the key trends driving this transformation are Artificial Intelligence (AI) and Machine Learning (ML). AI and ML are transforming traditional ERP systems by enabling intelligent automation, predictive analytics, and decision-making capabilities. With AI, ERP systems can analyze vast amounts of data, identify patterns, and make data-driven recommendations for optimized processes and improved business outcomes. ML algorithms allow ERP systems to learn from data and improve over time, enabling them to automate routine tasks, detect anomalies, and provide valuable insights for strategic decision-making. The integration of AI and ML into ERP technology holds the potential to enhance operational efficiency, optimize resource allocation, and drive innovation across various industries.

2. Big Data

Another significant emerging trend in ERP technology is the utilization of Big Data. With the increasing volume, variety, and velocity of data generated by businesses, harnessing and analyzing this data has become crucial for informed decision-making. ERP systems are incorporating Big Data capabilities to effectively capture, process, and analyze large and complex datasets from various sources. By leveraging Big Data analytics, ERP systems can uncover valuable insights, identify trends, and make more accurate predictions, leading to better strategic planning and improved operational efficiency. The integration of Big Data capabilities in ERP technology enables organizations to unlock the potential of their data assets and gain a competitive edge in today's data-driven business landscape.

3. Internet of Things (IoT)

The Internet of Things (IoT) is another emerging trend that is transforming ERP technology. IoT refers to the network of interconnected physical devices, sensors, and software that collect and exchange data over the internet. In the context of ERP, IoT enables the integration of real-time data from various devices and sensors into the ERP system. This data can include information about production equipment, supply chain logistics, inventory levels, and customer behavior. By leveraging IoT in ERP, organizations can gain real-time visibility into their operations, automate processes, improve asset tracking, and enhance decision-making. IoT integration with ERP systems allows for proactive monitoring, predictive maintenance, and optimization of resources, leading to improved operational efficiency and cost savings. As IoT technology continues to advance, its integration with ERP will further enable organizations to leverage the power of connected devices and drive digital transformation across various industries.

4. Cloud Computing

Cloud computing is a significant emerging trend in ERP technology. It involves the delivery of computing services over the internet, providing on-demand access to a shared pool of resources, such as servers, storage, and applications. Cloud-based ERP solutions are gaining popularity due to their scalability, flexibility, and cost-effectiveness. Organizations can leverage cloud computing to deploy ERP systems without the need for extensive on-premise infrastructure. This allows for faster implementation, reduced upfront costs, and simplified maintenance and upgrades. Cloud-based ERP also offers the advantage of remote accessibility, enabling users to access the system anytime and anywhere using internet-connected devices. Cloud computing provides robust data security measures, backup and recovery options, and high system availability. As the demand for agility, mobility, and cost-efficiency continues to grow, cloud-based ERP solutions are expected to become the preferred choice for organizations seeking modern and scalable ERP technology.

5. Blockchain Technology

Blockchain technology is an emerging trend in ERP that has the potential to transform the way transactions and data are recorded and managed. With its decentralized and immutable nature, blockchain offers enhanced security, transparency, and trust in ERP systems. It provides a distributed ledger where transactions are recorded and verified by multiple participants, eliminating the need for intermediaries and reducing the risk of fraud or tampering. Blockchain can be leveraged in ERP to streamline supply chain processes, track product provenance, and facilitate secure and transparent financial transactions. By utilizing smart contracts, ERP systems can automate and enforce contractual agreements, ensuring accurate and timely execution of business processes. As organizations increasingly prioritize data integrity, security, and trust, blockchain technology holds immense promise in revolutionizing the way ERP systems handle data, transactions, and collaborations.

6. Augmented reality, and virtual reality

Another emerging trend in ERP technology is the integration of augmented reality (AR) and virtual reality (VR) capabilities. AR and VR technologies provide immersive and interactive experiences, allowing users to visualize and interact with virtual elements in the real world. In the context of ERP systems, AR and VR can be used to enhance various processes, such as product design, training, and maintenance. For example, employees can use AR to visualize 3D models of products and simulate their assembly process, leading to more efficient production. VR can be utilized for virtual training sessions, enabling employees to learn and practice complex tasks in a safe and simulated environment. The integration of AR and VR in ERP systems can improve user engagement, enhance collaboration, and streamline operations, ultimately driving productivity and innovation.

Potential impact of emerging technologies on ERP systems

The influence of emerging technologies on ERP systems is substantial, with cloud computing, AI, and the IoT transforming the design, implementation, and utilization of ERP systems. Cloud computing revolutionizes accessibility and affordability, as cloud-based ERP systems eliminate the need for businesses to invest in hardware and software infrastructure, resulting in significant cost savings.

AI and ML introduce automation and enhanced decision-making capabilities to ERP systems. AI automates tasks like data entry and customer service, while ML analyzes data patterns and generates predictions to improve decision-making processes.

The IoT enables real-time data collection by connecting devices, offering opportunities to enhance efficiency, productivity, and customer service within ERP systems. For instance, inventory and equipment tracking through IoT can optimize supply chain management and logistics.

Emerging technologies such as blockchain, augmented reality (AR), and virtual reality (VR) have the potential to impact ERP systems. Blockchain ensures secure and transparent supply chains, while AR and VR provide employees with immersive training and support experiences.

The potential impact of these emerging technologies on ERP systems is extensive, as they enhance accessibility, affordability, and functionality. This enables businesses to enhance their efficiency, productivity, and customer service. As these technologies continue to evolve, we can anticipate further innovative and disruptive applications within ERP systems.

Future of ERP implementation and maintenance

The future of implementing and maintaining ERP systems is on the brink of significant changes driven by technological advancements and evolving business needs. With the growing adoption of digital transformation, ERP solutions must adapt to emerging trends and evolving requirements.

One pivotal aspect of future ERP implementation revolves around the surge of cloud-based solutions. Cloud computing offers advantages such as scalability, flexibility, and cost-effectiveness, making it an appealing choice for organizations of all sizes. The shift towards cloud-based ERP implementation will continue to expand, enabling businesses to access their ERP systems remotely, streamline operations, and leverage advanced analytics capabilities.

Another crucial facet of the future of ERP implementation and maintenance involves the integration of emerging technologies. AI, ML, and robotic process automation (RPA) will assume increasingly significant roles in automating processes, enhancing decision-making, and improving overall system performance. These technologies will empower ERP systems to intelligently process and analyze vast amounts of data, deliver real-time insights, and automate routine tasks, resulting in heightened efficiency and productivity.

The future of ERP implementation and maintenance will place a greater emphasis on user experience and user-friendliness. ERP vendors will prioritize designing intuitive interfaces, enhancing mobile accessibility, and incorporating user-centric design principles. This focus on user experience will empower end-users to interact more effectively with ERP systems, leading to higher adoption rates and improved overall user satisfaction.

ERP systems for Industry 4.0

Industry 4.0 refers to the fourth industrial revolution, characterized by the integration of advanced technologies into manufacturing processes. It encompasses the use of technologies such as the IoT, AI, big data analytics, and automation to create smart, interconnected, and data-driven manufacturing systems. Industry 4.0 aims to revolutionize the way products are designed, produced, and delivered, leading to increased efficiency, productivity, and innovation in the manufacturing sector.

ERP play a crucial role in supporting the implementation of Industry 4.0 initiatives. Industry 4.0, also known as the Fourth

Industrial Revolution, represents the integration of advanced technologies such as the Internet of Things (IoT), artificial intelligence (AI), big data analytics, and automation in the manufacturing sector. ERP for Industry 4.0 are designed to enable intelligent and connected manufacturing processes, optimizing operations and driving innovation.

One key aspect of ERP for Industry 4.0 is their ability to facilitate real-time data integration and analysis. With the IoT, various devices and sensors are interconnected, generating a vast amount of data. ERP collect, process, and analyze this data, providing valuable insights for decision-making and enabling predictive maintenance, supply chain optimization, and quality control. By leveraging AI and big data analytics capabilities, ERP help manufacturers identify patterns, detect anomalies, and make data-driven decisions, leading to improved efficiency, reduced downtime, and enhanced productivity.

ERP for Industry 4.0 support seamless integration and collaboration across the entire value chain. They enable connectivity between different departments, suppliers, and facilitate automated workflows. They also enhance communication and collaboration by providing shared platforms for data sharing, project management, and communication, fostering a more agile and responsive manufacturing ecosystem.

ERP systems for sustainable business practices

ERP play a vital role in supporting businesses' commitment to sustainability by providing effective tools for managing and monitoring their environmental and social impact. These offer functionalities that enable the tracking and analysis of essential sustainability metrics, including energy usage, waste generation, carbon emissions, and adherence to social compliance standards. By integrating sustainability data into the ERP system, organizations gain valuable insights to optimize resource utilization, minimize waste, and reduce their overall environmental footprint.

ERP promote supply chain transparency and traceability, empowering organizations to ensure ethical sourcing practices and responsible manufacturing. Modules such as supplier management and product lifecycle management are seamlessly integrated into ERP systems, allowing businesses to monitor suppliers' adherence to sustainability standards and certifications. This fosters the sourcing of raw materials from sustainable and socially responsible suppliers, upholds fair labor practices, and ensures compliance with environmental regulations. With the ability to capture and analyze sustainability-related data, ERP equip organizations with the necessary information to identify improvement areas, establish sustainability objectives, and evaluate progress towards achieving sustainable business practices.

Challenges and opportunities for ERP vendors and users in the future

In the future, ERP vendors and users will encounter various challenges and possibilities due to the ongoing evolution of technology. One notable challenge is the need to keep pace with the rapid advancements in technology. As emerging technologies like AI, IoT, and blockchain become more prevalent, ERP vendors must adapt their systems to effectively incorporate and utilize these technologies. This requires investments in research and development to stay ahead of the curve and provide innovative solutions that address the changing demands of users.

Another challenge lies in ensuring the security and privacy of data. With the increasing volume of data generated and processed by ERP systems, safeguarding sensitive information becomes crucial. ERP vendors and users must implement robust security measures, including encryption, access controls, and regular audits, to protect data from breaches and unauthorized access. Additionally, compliance with data protection regulations, such as GDPR, introduces an additional layer of complexity that vendors and users must navigate.

These challenges also present opportunities for ERP vendors and users. Embracing emerging technologies and integrating them into ERP systems can yield significant benefits. For vendors, it opens up new possibilities for innovation and differentiation, enabling them to offer advanced features and enhance user experiences. Users can leverage these technologies to streamline their processes, gain valuable insights from data analytics, automate repetitive tasks, and improve decision-making capabilities. The increasing adoption of cloud-based ERP solutions provides scalability, flexibility, and cost-effectiveness, empowering both vendors and users to leverage the advantages of cloud computing and access ERP systems from anywhere.

The future holds both challenges and opportunities for ERP vendors and users. By embracing technological advancements, prioritizing data security, and capitalizing on the benefits of cloud-based solutions, vendors can maintain their competitive edge and deliver ERP systems that bring added value. Users, on the other hand, can harness these advancements to optimize their business operations, gain a competitive advantage, and drive growth and success in an increasingly digital and interconnected world.

Conclusion and outlook

ERP have become indispensable tools for businesses, streamlining operations, improving efficiency, and enabling data-driven decision-making. The future of ERP holds exciting possibilities with advancements in technologies like artificial intelligence, machine learning, and the Internet of Things. We can expect intelligent automation, predictive analytics, and real-time insights to empower businesses to stay agile and innovative. Cloud-based ERP solutions will continue to gain popularity, offering scalability, flexibility, and cost-effectiveness. ERP will play a crucial role in helping organizations navigate the complexities of modern business and achieve their strategic objectives. The future of ERP is promising, presenting opportunities for businesses to optimize processes, enhance collaboration, and unlock their full potential.

11

Factors Affecting ERP Project Success

In this last section, we are going to explore the factors that can either contribute to or hinder the success of ERP projects. By examining these critical factors, we can gain insights into the key elements that play a significant role in the successful implementation of ERP systems. We will delve into aspects such as project planning, stakeholder engagement, change management, organizational readiness, and effective communication. Understanding these factors will enable us to identify potential challenges and develop strategies to overcome them, ultimately increasing the likelihood of a successful ERP project.

Introduction

The successful implementation of an ERP project holds significant importance for organizations, as it directly impacts their overall performance and operational efficiency. ERP systems provide a centralized platform that integrates various business functions, such as finance, human resources, supply chain, and customer relationship management, into a unified system. By streamlining processes, automating tasks, and providing real-time data insights,

ERP systems enable organizations to enhance productivity, reduce costs, and improve decision-making.

A successful ERP project implementation can bring several benefits to an organization. It enables better visibility and transparency across departments, facilitating smoother collaboration and coordination. This integration of data and processes eliminates information silos, reduces duplication of efforts, and enhances data accuracy. As a result, organizations can make informed decisions based on accurate, real-time information, leading to improved operational efficiency and faster response times.

Successful ERP implementation enables organizations to optimize their resource allocation, improve inventory management, and enhance supply chain visibility. By streamlining workflows and automating repetitive tasks, ERP systems free up valuable employee time, allowing them to focus on strategic initiatives and value-added activities. This increased efficiency and productivity translate into better customer service, higher customer satisfaction, and increased competitiveness in the marketplace.

We will explore the factors that can significantly impact the success of ERP projects.

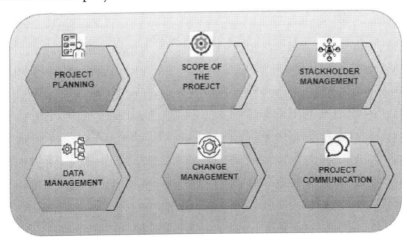

Figure 6. Key factors for ensuring a successful ERP project

Project Planning and Management

Comprehensive project planning and effective project management are crucial for the success of ERP implementation. Through clear goals, realistic timelines, resource allocation, and risk management, organizations can establish a strong foundation aligned with their strategic vision. Project managers play a critical role in coordinating teams, fostering communication, and monitoring progress, while actively mitigating risks and resolving issues. By combining these practices, organizations can navigate the complexities of ERP implementation, increasing the likelihood of achieving desired outcomes and driving positive business transformation.

Stakeholder Engagement

Stakeholder engagement is a critical factor in the success of ERP projects. Engaging key stakeholders, including executives, end-users, IT staff, and consultants, throughout the project lifecycle ensures effective communication, involvement, and buy-in. By involving stakeholders in decision-making and addressing their concerns, organizations can increase support and alignment, leading to a higher likelihood of successful ERP implementation. Effective stakeholder engagement fosters collaboration and ownership, helping to overcome challenges and drive project success.

Organizational Readiness

Organizational readiness is a key factor in the success of ERP implementation. Assessing the organization's culture, change readiness, and process maturity helps identify barriers and challenges. By developing effective change management strategies, organizations can overcome resistance and ensure a smooth transition to the new ERP system.

Change Management

Change management plays a crucial role in the success of ERP projects. It involves creating a comprehensive change management plan that addresses the impact of the new ERP system on employees, processes, and organizational culture. This includes identifying and addressing resistance to change, providing training and support to help employees adapt to the new system, and ensuring effective communication to foster acceptance and adoption. By actively managing the human side of the implementation process, organizations can minimize disruption, increase employee engagement, and maximize the benefits of the ERP system.

Technical Considerations

Technical considerations are crucial for the success of ERP projects. Careful planning and execution are necessary for integrating the ERP system with existing systems and migrating data smoothly. Assessing the organization's infrastructure readiness and ensuring scalability are important factors to support the ERP system's requirements effectively. By addressing these technical considerations, organizations can mitigate risks, avoid setbacks, and achieve a successful ERP implementation that aligns with their technical requirements and supports their business operations effectively.

Vendor Selection and Collaboration

Vendor selection and collaboration are vital for the success of ERP projects. The right ERP vendor should be chosen based on criteria such as functionality, scalability, and support. Contract negotiation establishes clear expectations and deliverables. Ongoing collaboration ensures alignment and effective communication. By focusing on vendor selection and fostering a collaborative partnership, organizations can maximize the success of their ERP projects.

Lessons Learned from Failed ERP Projects

Lessons learned from failed ERP projects provide valuable insights into common pitfalls, challenges, and mistakes that organizations should avoid. By analyzing case studies and real-world examples, organizations can identify factors that contribute to project failure, such as poor planning, inadequate stakeholder engagement, insufficient change management, and technical issues. These lessons help organizations understand the importance of comprehensive project planning, effective stakeholder communication and involvement, robust change management strategies, and addressing technical considerations. By learning from past failures, organizations can increase the chances of success in their own ERP projects and ensure a smooth and successful implementation that delivers the desired outcomes and benefits.

Success Stories and Best Practices

Examining success stories of organizations with successful ERP implementations provides valuable inspiration and guidance for similar projects. Effective project management, stakeholder engagement, change management, and organizational readiness are key factors contributing to success. By implementing comprehensive planning, engaging stakeholders, managing change, and assessing readiness, organizations can enhance their own ERP projects and increase their chances of success.

Conclusion and Outlook

The factors discussed in this chapter highlight the critical elements that can help or hinder the success of ERP projects. Comprehensive project planning, effective stakeholder engagement, organizational readiness, change management, technical considerations, and vendor collaboration all play pivotal roles in ensuring a successful ERP implementation. By learning from the lessons of failed projects and studying success stories, organizations can apply best practices to increase the likelihood of achieving their desired outcomes. Looking ahead, the future of ERP project success lies in embracing emerging trends and technologies, such as AI, machine learning, and cloud-based solutions. Continuous learning, adaptability, and a proactive mindset will be essential in navigating the evolving landscape and maximizing the benefits of ERP implementations. By prioritizing these factors and staying abreast of industry advancements, organizations can position themselves for success in their future ERP projects.

References

1) Critical factors for successful ERP implementation: Exploratory findings from four case studies by Jaideep Motwani, Ram Subramanian, Pradeep Gopalakrishna; (doi:10.1016/j.compind.2005.02.005)
2) ERP Failure in Developing Countries: A Case Study in India by Sheshadri Chatterjee; Center of Excellence, Cyber Systems and Information Assurance Indian Institute of Technology, sheshadri.academic@gmail.com
3) Learning from a failed ERP implementation: a case study research C. Venugopal and K. Suryaprakasa Rao Anna University, Chennai, India; DOI 10.1108/17538371111164038
4) Learning from a failed ERP implementation: The case of a large South African organization Anjali Ramburn, Lisa Seymour, Avinaash Gopaul University of Cape Town, Cape Town, South Africa Ranjali17@gmail.com
5) Successful implementation of ERP projects: Evidence from two case studies Jaideep Motwania, Dinesh Mirchandanib , Manu Madanc, A. Gunasekaran; motwanij@gvsu.edu; mirch-and@gvsu.edu; mirch-and@gvsu.edu; Agunasekaran@umassd.edu.
6) T. Gutmann, D. Kanbach, and S. Seltman, "Exploring the benefits of corporate accelerators: Investigating the SAP Industry 4.0 Startup program," Probl. Perspect. Manag., vol. 17, no. 3, pp. 218–232, 2019, doi: 10.21511/ppm.17(3).2019.18.
7) "SAP Business One:The Ultimate ERP Solution For Small And Mid-Sized Business - Saptutorials.in." https://www.saptutorials.in/sap-business-one-sap-for-small-business/.

8) "Oracle Cloud Applications ETL - Extracting Data from Oracle Cloud ERP." https://www.orbitanalytics.com/extracting-data-for-data-warehouses-from-oracle-cloud-erp/.
9) "Microsoft Dynamics 365: Integrated Cloud Solutions." https://dynatechconsultancy.com/what-is-microsoft-dynamics-365/.
10) K. Purandare, "Tally Solutions: Creating A Culture Of Care," Forbes India, Mar. 2022. [Online]. Available: https://www.forbesindia.com/article/india039s-best-employers-2022/tally-solutions-creating-a-culture-of-care/74197/1
11) "Understanding Enterprise Resource Planning (ERP)." https://www.ramco.com/blog/understanding-enterprise-resource-planning-erp.
12) Infor, "Infor M3 | ERP Solutions for Enterprise Manufacturers | Infor," 2019. https://www.infor.com/solutions/erp/m3.
13) "QAD Adaptive ERP Overview | Cloud-Based ERP System for Adaptive Manufacturing Enterprises." https://www.qad.com/ja-JP/data-sheets/qad-adaptive-erp.
14) "ERP, CRM & HCM Solutions for Various Industries in India." https://www.focussoftnet.com/in/.
15) "Epicor Business Architecture | Epicor ERP | ICE Tools | Manuacturing Technology." https://encompass-inc.com/epicor-business-architecture/.
16) "SAGE ERP - ACES, INC. Sage 300." https://aces.com.ph/sage300-erp.html.

Printed by Amazon Italia Logistica S.r.l.
Torrazza Piemonte (TO), Italy